The Baby Snooks Scripts

Vol. 2

By Philip Rapp

Edited by Ben Ohmart

THE BABY SNOOKS SCRIPTS VOL. 2 BY PHILIP RAPP

© 2007 Paul Rapp

All rights reserved.
No part of this book may be reproduced in any form or by any means, electronic, mechanical, digital, photocopying or recording, except for the inclusion in a review, without permission in writing from the the publisher.

Published in the USA by Bear Manor Media
PO Box 71426
Albany, GA 31708

www.Bearmanormedia.com
1-800-566-1251 (Order line only)

ISBN10: 1-59393-094-1
ISBN13: 978-1-59393-094-3

Printed in the United States

Cover Design by Joel Bogart (www.bogartsltd.com)
Book Design by SUN Editing & Book Design (suneditwrite.com)

Table of Contents

"GOOD NEWS OF 1939" — January 12, 1939 1

"GOOD NEWS OF 1939" — January 26, 1939 39

"GOOD NEWS OF 1940" — February 1, 1940 65

"GOOD NEWS OF 1940" — February 8, 1940 85

"MAXWELL HOUSE COFFEE TIME" — March 26, 1942 107

"MAXWELL HOUSE COFFEE TIME" — June 19, 1941 133

"GOOD NEWS OF 1940" — JULY 18, 1940 153

"GOOD NEWS OF 1940" — JULY 25, 1940 173

"LET'S LAUGH, LET'S SING" 193

"LITTLE OLIVE" 207

"UNCLE HITCHY AND LITTLE ALFRED" 223

Editor's Note

There are three reasons you're holding this book right now. Apart from the fact that you paid for it, of course. 1. The response to the first volume of Baby Snooks scripts was so great that there just had to be a sequel. 2. Unlike The Bickersons, which Phil Rapp wrote and directed for a number of years in a number of mediums, Rapp penned enough Snooks material for about 10 volumes. 3. This stuff is just too good to hide away in an archive somewhere. The ever-groaning Daddy with his stupefying vocabulary trying to convince his questioning daughter of his mental agility when he should just give a resounding "Shut up already!"—how could the formula miss?

Rapp must've written this stuff in Ziplock bags—it stays fresh year after year. Take out some of the occasional, dated WWII and rationing humor and you've got a wonderful set of comedy gems here that would make grandma and grandchild alike laugh out loud today. Much more of the success is due to the agile timing and cleverness of its true star, Hanley Stafford, I think, than the infamous Snooks, AKA Fanny Brice. But it really is the material that stars and spanks and crackles with corn and familial wit. If there is a fine line drawn between dated and timeless, the pencil is not pressed too hard in this volume.

Philip Rapp conquered film and television and radio, and though he'll always be known for pitting Frances Langford against snoring Don Ameche in their Bickersons bed, Baby Snooks lays claim to Rapp's universal appeal.

I just hope enough people buy this book so we can put out the other 8 volumes.

—Ben Ohmart
June 2007

MAXWELL HOUSE
Presents
"GOOD NEWS OF 1939"
January 12, 1939
#55

CAST

1. Warren Hull
2. Robert Young
3. Dennis O'Keefe
4. Nat Pendleton
5. Cecelia Parker
6. Tony Martin
7. Frank Morgan
8. Fanny Brice
9. Hanley Stafford
10. Meredith Willson and Orchestra
11. Max Terr Chorus

1	(OPENING) ("JOOBALAI" —BAND)
2 - 2B	(YOUNG - WILLSON - MARTIN - HULL) ("OUT OF NOWHERE" —MARTIN)
3 - 3E	BABY SNOOKS
4 - 4A	COMMERCIAL
5 - 5C	(YOUNG - MORGAN - KORJUS) ("AH FORS' E LUI" —KORJUS)
6 - 6E	MORGAN
7	STATION BREAK
8	"YOU MUST HAVE BEEN A BEAUTIFUL BABY" —BAND

9 - 9G   PREVIEW: "BURN 'EM UP O'CONNOR" —O'KEEFE - PENDLETON - PARKER

10   "I CRIED FOR YOU" —MARTIN

11 - 11A   SNOOKS POEM: "THREE LITTLE KITTENS"

12 - 12A   COMMERCIAL

13   CONCERT HALL: "SONG OF INDIA" —KORJUS

14 - 14F   "IF MEN WENT APARTMENT HUNTING AS WOMEN DO" —YOUNG - MORGAN - WILLSON - STAFFORD

15 - 15A   CLOSING

HULL: Maxwell House Coffee presents … Good News of 1939!

(MUSIC IN AND FADE)

HULL: The makers of Maxwell House Coffee welcome you to another hour of music and gaiety with your favorite screen stars, from the famous Metro-Goldwyn-Mayer Studios in Hollywood. And here is your host for the evening — Robert Young!

(APPLAUSE … MUSIC OUT)

YOUNG: Thank you, Warren — good evening, everybody. Just to set your minds at rest, I'd like to make one announcement right away. If you were with us last week, you may remember that we opened the program with a number in which I — well, I sang it. Well, I didn't exactly sing it. That is, I threatened to sing it, and as a matter of fact I did sing a little of it, but the stalwart MGM chorus here — 12 people, mostly girls — were able to drown me out. Anyhow, tonight I won't sing at all.

But just in case that announcement should disappoint some of you — which seems doubtful — let me tell you who IS going to sing on our show tonight. The most exciting new singing star of the year, the lovely Viennese lady who thrilled you all in *The Great Waltz*

—Miliza Korjus! Other guests I'm sure you will enjoy are the cast of Hollywood's surprise preview of the past week, our new drama of the auto racing game, "Burn 'Em Up O'Connor." You'll meet Dennis O'Keefe, Cecelia Parker, and Nat Pendleton.

All this, of course, is in addition to Fanny Brice and Hanley Stafford, Frank Morgan, Tony Martin and Meredith Willson and his orchestra. Meredith starts off now with a new rhythm number, Joobalai.

Whenever you're ready, Meredith.

"JOOBALAI" —ORCHESTRA

(APPLAUSE)

YOUNG:	That was very good, Meredith.
MEREDITH:	Thank you, old fellow. Say — have you noticed anything peculiar about Frank Morgan?
YOUNG:	I always do. That's what makes him Frank Morgan.
MEREDITH:	No, I mean tonight. And he isn't acting peculiar like he usually does. He's acting peculiar in a new way, and that's what seemed peculiar.
YOUNG:	Oh. But you're all right, huh? Listen, Meredith — what did Frank do that struck you as out of the ordinary?
MEREDITH:	Well — he usually doesn't notice me at all — but tonight he seemed very friendly — and — well, I promised him I wouldn't tell.
YOUNG:	Aw — come on, Dithy! You can tell your chum!
MEREDITH:	(PROP LAUGH) You won't let it go any farther?
YOUNG:	Not an inch. Your secret dies with me, Dithy.
MEREDITH:	Frank gave me an absolutely sure tip on the fifth race today. If the odds are as good as he says, I'll probably make a lot of money.
YOUNG:	Oh, sure. What's the name of the horse, Meredith?

MEREDITH: (VERY CONFIDENTIAL) The name of the horse is —Blue Bolt.

YOUNG: (VERY QUIET ECHO) Blue Bolt.

MEREDITH: Blue Bolt. An absolute cinch.

YOUNG: Meredith, I can only give you one piece of advice. Don't bet any money on the horse.

MEREDITH: But, Bob — it's a sure thing! I bet ten dollars on it!

YOUNG: Ten dollars!

MEREDITH: Yes — and of course another ten for Frank.

YOUNG: I see. Was that Frank's idea?

MEREDITH: Er — I don't think so. He may have dropped some remark about a bet for *him* making *me* lucky. Yes — that was it. The one for him is a luck bet.

YOUNG: A luck bet. You'll need it, kid.

MEREDITH: Thanks, Bob. Now don't tell anybody — promise!

YOUNG: Don't worry. (MEREDITH GOES) Well, ladies and gentlemen, you can see what's going on here. But we'd better be getting on with the show. Our next—

HULL: Excuse me, Bob.

YOUNG: What's the matter, Warren?

HULL: Do you mind if I use this phone? Tony Martin's using the booth out in the hall.

YOUNG: Well - I suppose it's all right. Something urgent?

HULL: Urgent? I'll say it's urgent. I've got a sure thing in the fifth race and I want to make a bet.

YOUNG: Warren — did you get a tip from Frank Morgan?

HULL: Er — yes.

YOUNG: (SOTTO VOICE) Blue Bolt?

HULL: Oh no! He gave me a sure winner — (SOTTO VOICE) — Yellow Jack.

YOUNG: (LOUD...SURPRISED) Yellow Jack!

HULL: Shhhh!

YOUNG: (SOTTO) Yellow Jack?

HULL: (SOTTO) Yellow Jack. He's in the bag. So I just want to get a little bet down. Ten for me and ten for Frank — a little luck bet.

YOUNG: I'm beginning to see which way the luck is running. Well, go ahead and use the phone, if you want to — no, wait a minute, here comes Tony Martin, you can use the booth now.

HULL: Okay.

YOUNG: Hi, Tony! Gee, it's swell to have you back!

TONY: Great to be back, Bob! And I really mean it! What's come over everybody?

YOUNG: I don't know — what do you mean, Tony?

TONY: Well — Frank Morgan never paid much attention to me before —

YOUNG: Here it comes.

TONY: But he just gave me a dead cinch for the fifth race.

YOUNG: See if I can guess. It wasn't Blue Bolt.

TONY: No.

YOUNG: And it wasn't Yellow Jack.

TONY: No. I'll give him to you, Bob — but don't let it get around. You know — force the odds down.

YOUNG: Don't worry, kid.

TONY: The name of the horse is — (SOTTO VOICE) Green Goddess.

YOUNG:	(SOTTO) Green Goddess.
TONY:	(SOTTO) Green Goddess. He's in the bag—and when he comes in he'll be carrying twenty bucks of mine on his back!
YOUNG:	Twenty!
TONY:	Sh! Ten for me and ten for Frank.
YOUNG:	Oh, the luck bet, sure! Well, Tony, my advice to you is to sing, and sing good, so you'll keep working. What have you got for us tonight?
TONY:	Bob, it's an oldie, but it's a goodie. Remember a tune of Johnny Green's called "Out of Nowhere?"
YOUNG:	Sure! That's where Morgan gets his horses! Take it, Tony!
	"OUT OF NOWHERE" —MARTIN & ORCHESTRA
	(APPLAUSE)
YOUNG:	Nice going, Tony! Stick around; we'll need you again later!
TONY:	Okay, Bob!
YOUNG:	Now here she is, ladies and gentlemen, Fanny Brice as Baby Snooks!
	(MUSIC ... APPLAUSE)
YOUNG:	Daddy, played by Hanley Stafford, has just returned from the office and is sitting quietly in his study engrossed in the evening newspaper. Listen.
FATHER:	(A LOT OF SATISFIED GRUNTS)
SOUND:	(DOOR SLAM)
BRICE:	(EXCITED) Lookit, daddy!
FATHER:	(GRUNTS ABSTRACTEDLY) Hmm — go away, Snooks.

BRICE: Lookit what I got!

FATHER: (GRUNTS) I'm reading, Snooks!

BRICE: I got a fishy! (LAUGHS)

FATHER: Huh? Wha — SNOOKS! Put that fish in some water!

BRICE: Why?

FATHER: Because it'll die in your hands! Where'd you get it?

BRICE: I tooked it from the pond in the park.

FATHER: The park? You carried the goldfish all the way home in your hands?

BRICE: Uh-huh. Ain't it pretty?

FATHER: How on earth did it stay alive out of the water?

BRICE: I kept spittin' on it!

FATHER: PUT THAT GOLDFISH IN WATER! Here — slip it in this glass.

BRICE: Awight … (LAUGHS) … It's swimming!

FATHER: All right — leave it alone. I want to read. (GRUNTS)

BRICE: Daddy?

FATHER: What is it?

BRICE: The fish is hungry.

FATHER: (CURT) Feed it.

BRICE: Gimme a penny and I'll buy a lollipop.

FATHER: Fish don't like lollipops!

BRICE: I like 'em.

FATHER: Well, you can't have one. Let me read!

BRICE: Awight … Daddy?

FATHER: What?

BRICE: What do fishies eat?

FATHER: I don't know. Big fish eat little fish.

BRICE: Does whales eat goldfish?

FATHER: No — any fish but goldfish.

BRICE: Does whales eat sardines?

FATHER: Yes!

BRICE: How do they open the *cans*?

FATHER: When fish are in the water they're not in cans. They swim around in schools.

BRICE: Goldfish, too?

FATHER: Yes — goldfish swim in schools.

BRICE: This one wasn't in school.

FATHER: That's probably why you caught it — and it serves him right!

BRICE: For playing hookey?

FATHER: NO! Let me read my paper! Can't I get a minute's peace in this house?

BRICE: I won't bother you, daddy.

FATHER: All right … (GRUNTS AND SETTLES)

BRICE: Daddy!

FATHER: Now what is it?

BRICE: I think the fish is gonna drown.

FATHER: Don't be silly.

BRICE: He's got his mouth open.

FATHER: He's breathing.

BRICE: In the water?

FATHER:	Yes. Fish open their mouths, take in a quantity of water, and by a chemical process they extract the oxygen from it and expel the rest thru their gills.
BRICE:	Is it hard?
FATHER:	No! Any fish can do it.
BRICE:	Let me see you do it, daddy.
FATHER:	I'm not a fish!
BRICE:	Why?
FATHER:	Why? Because if I were a fish you'd be a fish too!
BRICE:	Why?
FATHER:	Because human beings don't have fish!
BRICE:	We had fish Friday!
FATHER:	We had fish for supper — but we don't have fish for children.
BRICE:	I had some.
FATHER:	Well, what of it?
BRICE:	Ain't I a children?
FATHER:	WILL YOU LET ME READ MY PAPER!
BRICE:	Awight ... Daddy?
FATHER:	Ohhh! What do you want?
BRICE:	Was I a fish when I was borned?
FATHER:	Stop those silly questions!
BRICE:	Did you have to take me — or did you pick me out?
FATHER:	We picked you out!
BRICE:	Why?
FATHER:	Oh, so *you're* beginning to wonder, too!

BRICE:	Huh?
FATHER:	Nothing! Let me read.
BRICE:	Read to me, daddy.
FATHER:	No!
BRICE:	Waaahhh!
FATHER:	(DEEP RESIGNED SIGH) Oh, well. Hand me that animal picture book — you might as well get a little lesson in zoology.
BRICE:	Here, daddy.
FATHER:	Now just don't ask too many questions and I'll be able to explain things to you.
BRICE:	Awight.
FATHER:	This whole book is in alphabetical order — see? Now, A stands for anteater — it's got a long snout, very slovenly in its habits, very heavy shapeless body, and hardly any brains at all. Here's the picture.
BRICE:	Uh-huh.
FATHER:	Now — what is it?
BRICE:	Uncle Louie.
FATHER:	No. I just told you! Ant — ant —
BRICE:	Aunt Sophie!
FATHER:	B stands for bear! See the bear? See his warm fur coat? He wears that all the time.
BRICE:	In summer too.
FATHER:	All the time.
BRICE:	Why don't he take it off?
FATHER:	Because he was made that way!

BRICE: Who made him?

FATHER: The — the angels!

BRICE: I can take my coat off!

FATHER: Sure you can — because you just find the buttons, open them up and take it off. Now — can the bear take off his warm fur coat?

BRICE: No.

FATHER: Why?

BRICE: 'Cause only the angels know where the buttons is!

FATHER: Oh, forget it! C stands for cat! I hope I don't have to tell you what a cat is!

BRICE: No, daddy.

FATHER: All right — you describe it.

BRICE: Huh?

FATHER: Describe it! What do cats have that no other animal has?

BRICE: Kittens.

FATHER: I see. Well, let's go to the next page. D stands for — do you know what this picture is?

BRICE: Uh-huh.

FATHER: Are you sure?

BRICE: Uh-huh.

FATHER: What is it?

BRICE: I dunno.

FATHER: I thought so! D stands for (SPELLS) D-E-E-R. What's that?

BRICE: Dog.

FATHER:	No! D-E-E-R! Look at that picture! What does mummy call me?
BRICE:	(LAUGHS)
FATHER:	What are you laughing at?
BRICE:	That ain't a *donkey*!
FATHER:	I'm gonna read. Go out of the room.
BRICE:	I don't wanna.
FATHER:	I'm warning you, Snooks.
BRICE:	I'm warning you, Snooks.
FATHER:	Leave me alone!
BRICE:	Leave me alone!
FATHER:	SNOOKS!
BRICE:	SNOOKS!
FATHER:	Will you stop mocking me?
BRICE:	Will you stop mocking me?
FATHER:	Oh, all right — I just won't talk.
BRICE:	Oh, all right — I just won't talk.
FATHER:	(GRUNTS)
BRICE:	(GRUNTS)
FATHER:	(COUGHS)
BRICE:	(COUGHS)
FATHER:	(YELLS) Stop it, I say!
BRICE:	(YELLS) Stop it, I say!
FATHER:	Snooks is a dope!
BRICE:	Snooks is a dope! … WAAAHHHH!

FATHER:	(WILD LAUGH) I got you! (LAUGHS)
BRICE:	WAAHHHH!
	(MUSIC ... APPLAUSE)
YOUNG:	Warren, whenever I see that enthusiastic light in your eye, I know it's time for a word from you on your favorite topic.
HULL:	And a favorite topic with most Americans, Bob, every day of the week. For good coffee contributes more to the enjoyment of living in this country than anywhere else in the world. That's why we're glad more and more people are finding pleasure and downright satisfaction in the *new* Maxwell House Coffee. Proud that more people, in fact, are buying Maxwell House than ever before in its history!
YOUNG:	I'm mighty proud to hear that, too, Warren. And I'm sure you can tell us why.
HULL:	We believe we do know why.
	Friends, from the day it was created more than half a century ago by that master coffee blender, Joel Cheek, Maxwell House has been known and appreciated as one of the world's finest coffees. Millions of people considered it just about perfect.
	But today, after months of effort and experimentation, we are able to say that this famous blend of superb coffees is now richer, more delicious, more full-bodied than ever before! You'll taste its extra goodness in your very first steaming, fragrant cup.
	Then, too, we think you'll appreciate that remarkable new "radiant roast" process we've developed, which roasts each coffee bean *evenly all the way through*, and so brings out the true, natural flavor of this superb new blend. No chance of bitter coffee due to parching, or weak coffee due to under-roasting.
	This new Maxwell House comes to you roaster-fresh in the same, familiar blue super-vacuum can, with all its

marvelous flavor and fragrance *sealed in*, none wasted. So if *you* haven't tried Maxwell House lately, won't you order a pound tomorrow? We think you'll say:

MAN'S VOICE: This is the finest coffee I've *ever* tasted!

HULL: We think you'll agree this *new* Maxwell House Coffee is more than ever … good to the last drop!

(MUSIC BRIDGE)

YOUNG - MORGAN - KORJUS

MORGAN: Oh — hello, Bob!

YOUNG: Frank! How are you?

MORGAN: Fine! Could I have a word with you, old man?

YOUNG: Why sure, Frank!

MORGAN: You've always been a good friend of mine.

YOUNG: I've tried to be.

MORGAN: I want to do you a favor.

YOUNG: That's mighty nice of you, Frank.

MORGAN: No trouble at all … Er — Bob, do you know anything about horses?

YOUNG: Not a thing — why?

MORGAN: Listen. (SOTTO VOICE) I want to give you an absolutely certain winner in the fifth race this afternoon.

YOUNG: A sure thing?

MORGAN: He'll come in like he was alone on the track.

YOUNG: What's the name of the horse, Frank?

MORGAN: (LOOKS AROUND) Don't tell anybody else — White Queen. He'll probably start at 30 to 1.

YOUNG:	White Queen, eh? Seems to me I've heard a lot about a horse named Blue Bolt.
MORGAN:	Blue Bolt? Blue Bolt hasn't got a chance.
YOUNG:	Oh. Well — then I heard some people talking about Yellow Jack.
MORGAN:	Yellow Jack? A truck horse, Bob. Shouldn't be allowed to race at all. White Queen is positively the only horse in the race.
YOUNG:	Well, gee, Frank, I'm much obliged to you. Of course, I never bet.
MORGAN:	You never — well of course I know you don't gamble, Bob — but when you bet on this horse you're really just investing your money. Ten dollars on this horse is like putting your money in government bonds. And when you make the bet, you can absolutely insure it by making what we call a luck bet.
YOUNG:	Oh — a luck bet. What's that, Frank?
MORGAN:	You bet ten dollars for yourself, and ten for me — that way, you can't lose! (GIGGLES)
YOUNG:	(LAUGHS WITH HIM) All right, Frank. I'll try to raise some money — and much obliged!
MORGAN:	Not at all, Bob — glad to do it for a friend! See you later! (HE GOES)
YOUNG:	Has he got a nerve! He must think all people are chumps. Well — ladies and gentlemen, we continue with — no — excuse me a minute.
SOUND:	(RATTLE PHONE RECEIVER)
YOUNG:	Let me have Crestview 1567, please. (PAUSE ... HE HUMS OR WHISTLES) Hello — let me speak to Mrs. Young, please — this is Mr. Young ... Hello dear. Say, I'm not going to bring Frank Morgan home to dinner tonight after all ... No, the fellow's too slick, I

don't want him in my house ... What did he do? Well, he just gave me a phony tip on a horse, and I don't want ... The name of the horse is White Queen, but what's the difference? Frank doesn't know anything. He's given four people on the program four different horses for the fifth race, and I don't want a fellow like that around my — ... You had a dream — ... so what? ... You dreamed our grass turned white and it looked wonderful? ... So you think we should bet on White Queen — ... Well, I don't think so — but of course if the horse should win, I'd certainly feel like a sap ... What's that? Of course, Frank MIGHT know something. Maybe I should put a little protection bet on him ... No — not two dollars. Make it ten ... Yes. And — er — another ten for Frank ... Sure. All right, Dear, I'll be home right after the show, and could we have Brussels sprouts for dinner? ... No, I hate 'em, but Frank likes 'em ... Yes, dear. Goodbye. (HANG UP PHONE) Well — ladies and gentlemen, I hope you'll pardon the interruption. It is now my pleasure to present the charming lady who became a star in *"The Great Waltz"* — Miss Miliza Korjus!

(APPLAUSE)

KORJUS: Thank you, Mr. Young. Could you tell me something, please?

YOUNG: Anything at all, Miss Korjus. At your service.

KORJUS: What is the name of the very charming gentleman I was talking to just now — outside?

YOUNG: Well — I don't know — which one?

KORJUS: Very distinguished looking. He looks like a man who used to have a mustache.

YOUNG: Oh, that's Frank Morgan! Yes, he used to have a mustache.

KORJUS: Mr. Morgan — he works for a horse racing track, no?

YOUNG:	Why, that unscrupulous — Did he tell you he worked for the horse racing track, Miss Korjus?
KORJUS:	No, but he knows which horse is going to win the fifth race today, and he told me.
YOUNG:	Just a minute. What's the name of the horse, Miss Korjus?
KORJUS:	Red Light. Don't tell — but will you do me a favor?
YOUNG:	Well, sure, but —
KORJUS:	Will you please bet on him for me … I do not know how to do it, please.
YOUNG:	Miss Korjus, I'd be delighted. I can kill Morgan afterwards. Would about twenty dollars be right?
KORJUS:	Exactly! Ten for me and ten for him. Now I sing, please.
YOUNG:	Yes. What are you going to sing?
KORJUS:	"Ah fors' e lui," from Traviata.
YOUNG:	Fine.

"AH FORS' E LUI" —KORJUS & ORCHESTRA

(APPLAUSE)

YOUNG:	That was beautiful, Miss Korjus! Now don't worry about that bet. I'll take care of it for you.
KORJUS:	Thank you so much!

MORGAN - YOUNG

STOOGE:	Say, Buddy, is Frank Morgan around here?
YOUNG:	I think so. Who wants to see him?
STOOGE:	Just tell him Harry. I'm his bookie.
YOUNG:	Oh. That's very interesting. Does Mr. Morgan win much money?

STOOGE:	Hasn't won a bet all season. He bets two dollars to show on the favorites, and he owes me sixteen dollars from yesterday.
YOUNG:	Yesterday — and you're here to collect it now?
STOOGE:	Listen, Buddy, you run your business, and I'll run mine. Where's Morgan?
YOUNG:	I'll get him. Oh Frank! Frank!
MORGAN:	Coming, Bob. What is it? Oh — what are you doing here?
STOOGE:	You know what I want.
MORGAN:	Oh — yes, well, you'll have to see me some other time. I can't talk about insurance today. Good morning.
STOOGE:	Good morning my neck! Give me that dough!
YOUNG:	Do you let your insurance man talk that way to you, Frank?
MORGAN:	That's my policy. (GIGGLES) Good day, sir.
STOOGE:	Gimme the money.
YOUNG:	(SOTTO) Harry, will you get out of here? How does it look, a man coming in here in front of all these people—
STOOGE:	(SOTTO) Gimme the dough, and I'll blow!
MORGAN:	Oh! (LOUD VOICE) All right, sir, here I've got a check all made out, and you can send the policy to my house.
STOOGE:	Oh, sure. So long, kid.
MORGAN:	These insurance men! Oh!
YOUNG:	Mm-hm. Since when does the Globe Life take bets on horses?
MORGAN:	Er — horses — Globe — did he say anything to you, Bob?

YOUNG: No. He just told me he was your bookmaker.

MORGAN: I've been kicked by a horse!

YOUNG: Frank, I don't know why you lie to me.

MORGAN: Well, I wouldn't want people to know — but I just gave him a check for eighty thousand dollars.

YOUNG: Eighty thousand dollars!

MORGAN: Just one bet — horse lost by a lip.

YOUNG: Listen, Tout — that tip you gave me on the fifth race — is that on the level?

MORGAN: Absolutely, Bob. You can depend on my tips. Wherever Morgan is, you'll find the dope … who said that?

YOUNG: I wish I had. Listen, Frank, that bookie told me you lost only sixteen dollars — where do you get that eighty thousand stuff?

MORGAN: Er — he's suffering from a very rare ailment. Fisticuff's disease.

YOUNG: Fisticuff's disease.

MORGAN: Yes — makes him want to reduce figures.

YOUNG: See what he can do for my Aunt Emma.

MORGAN: But actually there's not much thrill in horse racing, Bob.

YOUNG: No.

MORGAN: Not for a man who's lost fifty thousand francs on the turn of a card, the roll of a die, the spin of a wheel.

YOUNG: The Bulova watch time.

MORGAN: (LOOKS AT HIM) Young, you'll soon be in demand as a toastmaster at banquets. (HURT) Evidently you wouldn't care to hear about the time I broke the bank at Monte Carlo.

YOUNG: Aw, come on, Frank. I'd love to hear it.

MORGAN: All right. Some years ago, I decided to visit the French Riviera for my health.

YOUNG: Was your health bad?

MORGAN: No, it was excellent, but I wanted to improve it. I sailed from New York on the fifth of June, traveling light — only fifty-four pieces of luggage.

YOUNG: Traveling light. Fifty-four pieces.

MORGAN: A deck of playing cards and a pair of socks. I like to amuse myself playing solitaire. And sure enough, the boat had not been out five minutes before I was indulging in my favorite pastime.

YOUNG: Dry martinis?

MORGAN: Yes. NO! I was drinking an old fash— I mean I was playing solitaire! After a pleasant voyage, we docked at Cherbourg, and I went straight to the Riviera, and rented a gorgeous villa.

YOUNG: By the sea?

MORGAN: No, by the week. I wish you could have seen it, Bob. Downstairs, Louis the Fourteenth, upstairs, Louis the Fifteenth, in the attic, Louis Dubois.

YOUNG: Wait a minute. What's Louis Dubois?

MORGAN: He was the caretaker's brother — he lived up there with a goat. But not only the house, the whole countryside was beautiful, Bob. Lovely woodlands, abounding in all kinds of game. Ah, how I love to hunt!

YOUNG: What do you shoot?

MORGAN: Two dollars.

YOUNG: You're faded.

MORGAN: Seven.

YOUNG: The dice are loaded.

MORGAN: Yes. Well, I organized a hunting party, and —

YOUNG: Frank, will you get back to Monte Carlo and break the bank, please.

MORGAN: Don't be so impatient, Young! It's these little details that makes the story live!

YOUNG: (YAWNS) Go on, Frank!

MORGAN: I organized a hunting party with some of my neighbors, and on the third day, one of them shot a boar.

YOUNG: Show me the wound, Frank.

MORGAN: Callow urchin! Have you never heard the words of Seneca —

YOUNG: Sarcasm is the weapon of fools!

MORGAN: At any rate, with the outdoor life of the woodland, my health soon improved to a point where I craved diversion — one night about ten o'clock the blasé hangers-on of Monte Carlo sat up in their chairs as a handsome, faultlessly tailored young man, with the Legion of Honor across his shirt front, strode into the Casino. Inside of two hours, he had won a billion francs, and broken the bank.

YOUNG: It was you.

MORGAN: No. I was at the next table, and lost a dollar eighty. But this man's magnificent courage inspired me, Bob. During the night I pored over systems of roulette — during the day I poured out magnums of champagne. Finally I found it, Bob — Have you ever heard of the Stravinsky system of mathematical progression?

YOUNG: No.

MORGAN: It's infallible — and it's simplicity itself. The idea is to wait until red comes up on the wheel, and then play black three times in a row, doubling your stakes as you go along. Then you switch to red twice, and back to black, once. By this time, of course, your stakes have quadrupled, but when you reach the fifteen level, you divide by four and start at one.

YOUNG: With that, you cleaned up, huh?

MORGAN: Every night, I won fifty dollars. There was only one hitch in the system.

YOUNG: What was that?

MORGAN: It was costing me two hundred dollars a day to live.

YOUNG: A detail. Frank, when did you break the bank?

MORGAN: It was the night after I met the Countess. What a charming woman she was! Regal, too — in a democratic sort of way. (GIGGLES) When I first saw her, she was seated across the chemin de fer table from me, dissolved in tears.

YOUNG: The beauty was crying?

MORGAN: It touched me to the quick, Bob. I glanced at the other players in the game. There was ten thousand francs in the pool — and I cried Banco! The dealer flipped me a jack — a nine — and pushed the pile of money toward me. The crowd buzzed as I rose and said, "It is for Madame!" She looked up at me, her eyes filled with gratitude — stuffed the money into her evening bag, and rushed out of the Casino.

YOUNG: What followed?

MORGAN: I did.

YOUNG: Thought so.

MORGAN: I hurried after her, and saw her meet her husband in a little park near the Casino. She handed him the bank notes without a word. He sneered, and slapped her cheek. I boiled, and leaped toward them.

YOUNG:	Yes?
MORGAN:	I flung my glove in his face, and handed him my card.
YOUNG:	A duel!
MORGAN:	What else? Bob, it wasn't till morning I discovered my adversary was Count Prinzmetal, the finest swordsman in all Europe. But I'm pretty handy with the opoe myself, and we met behind the abbey with our seconds at dawn. We fought for two hours on the dewy grass, in the weird half-light of the Mediterranean sunrise — I won't give you the details, but they buried the Count where he fell.
YOUNG:	You ran him through?
MORGAN:	No, he tripped over a brick and broke his head. And the Countess — well, the Countess is now Mrs. George C. Smith of Chicago.
YOUNG:	I've got to hand it to you, Frank. You had a lot of nerve, going up against the finest duelist in Europe.
MORGAN:	Well — c'est la guerre! Bob — you see this little cicatrice here on my left cheek?
YOUNG:	Yes! I never noticed it before! A scar from the duel?
MORGAN:	No, I cut myself shaving this morning. Well, so long, boys, I gotta see a man about buying a safety razor!
	(MUSIC UP ... APPLAUSE)
	STATION BREAK COMMERCIAL
YOUNG:	Well, Warren, I need neither script, nor stopwatch, nor the expectant look on Meredith Willson's face to tell me what's next in the proceedings tonight. That wonderful fragrance in the air means only one thing —
HULL:	Right you are, Bob. Time right now for that familiar Thursday evening custom of ours ... a moment of relaxation over a steaming, freshly made cup of the *new* Maxwell House Coffee.

YOUNG:	And friends, we're inviting all of you everywhere to join us in this friendly custom in your own homes. We think you'll enjoy this show of ours still more over a cup of the coffee that's good to the last drop. And now, Warren, if you'll do the honors …
WILLSON:	Er, Bob … shall I pour out the music?
YOUNG:	Er, Meredith, pray do!
	(MUSIC UP AND FADE)
HULL:	We pause briefly for station identification.
	(MUSIC UP AND FADE)
YOUNG:	This is Bob Young again, and we start the second half of our Maxwell House Good News program with a new tune that's a big favorite all over the country — "You Must Have Been a Beautiful Baby." Play it, Meredith!
	"BEAUTIFUL BABY" —ORCHESTRA
	(APPLAUSE)

O'KEEFE - PARKER - PENDLETON - YOUNG - MORGAN

YOUNG:	Now, Ladies and Gentlemen, Maxwell House presents … A Hollywood success story. The kind of story that makes Hollywood, Hollywood — "A City of Dreams Come True" — if you're lucky. A little over a year ago, a young man walked onto the MGM lot to make a test for a bit part in "ROSALIE." Instead of this he found himself catapulted into one of the most important leads of the year and being hailed as Hollywood's newest discovery in romantic leading men. It all came about this way: Playing a bit part in "Saratoga" he came to the notice of Clark Gable and director Jack Conway who called him to the attention of studio executives. He was given a test and placed on the roster of MGM stock players. Now our scene shifts to Producer Harry Rapf who was looking for a leading man to work with Wally Beery and Virginia Bruce in "Bad Man of Brimstone."

When Mr. Rapf happened to see this young actor's screen test, he said, "That's my man!"

Next morning, this young man discovered that he was a "discovery." Now... may I introduce the hero of this little "thumbnail drama" ... my good friend ... DENNIS O'KEEFE!

(APPLAUSE)

O'KEEFE: Thanks, Bob... and thank you, ladies and gentlemen.

YOUNG: Well, Denny, how about you picking up with the story from where I left off...?

O'KEEFE: Bob, I think you just about covered the whole department.

YOUNG: Oh no... I mean let's start from a 'way back at the beginning. You know... the works...

O'KEEFE: Okay, Bob ... starting from way back ... my folks were known in vaudeville as Edward and Charlotte Flanagan, one of the finest teams that ever trouped the "Two-a-day." Later Dad teamed up with Neely Edwards and they played the circuits as "Flanagan and Edwards ..." Remember "THE HALL ROOM BOYS?"

YOUNG: I used to laugh my head off at them when I was a kid.

O'KEEFE: Well, Bob, before they were in pictures, I traveled with them all over the country, so you can see I was practically raised in a trunk. I've got vaudeville in my blood.

YOUNG: Oh. ... so that's where it went ... ?? Seriously, Denny... if your Dad was one of the Hall Room Boys... then Hollywood isn't a new thing with you?

O'KEEFE: Oh no... after dad went into pictures ... we settled out here and I went to school in Hollywood.

YOUNG: Denny, in those days did you ever think of becoming an actor?

O'KEEFE: Constantly, Bob. Constantly. High-school plays, church socials … community get-togethers, anything. Any time there was the remotest chance to emote … there was O'Keefe … 'rarin' to go!

YOUNG: I understand you also did a bit of vaudeville on your own.

O'KEEFE: Yes … but success in Hollywood was the "big" ambition, so I started trying. .. Many months of "extra" work … when I was lucky enough to get it … and finally Mr. Rapf came my way.

YOUNG: Which all goes to prove that Mr. Rapf used excellent judgment, because since "Bad Men of Brimstone" you've turned in some fine performances … and Denny, my scouts tell me that your new picture "Burn 'Em Up O'Connor" is really a killer-diller.

O'KEEFE: Bob … it's one of the fastest moving pictures I've ever been in. Based on a story by the great speed driver Sir Malcolm Campbell, it's full of thrills, spills and crashes that will have you on the edge of your chair, tense with excitement …

YOUNG: Well, Denny, you've got some darned nice people with you in "Burn 'Em Up O'Connor." Harry Carey… Alan Curtis … Nat Pendleton… Charley Grapewin …

O'KEEFE: And don't forget my leading lady, Bob. She's one of the sweetest, most talented and nicest girls on the MGM lot.

PARKER: Thank you, Dennis.

YOUNG: Well, Cecilia Parker!

(APPLAUSE)

PARKER: How are you, Bob?

YOUNG: Fine, Cecilia … as you've probably gathered … we're talking about "Burn 'Em Up O'Connor."

PARKER: Yes ... and take my word for it, Dennis is grand in the picture.

O'KEEFE: You're pretty swell in it, yourself, Cecilia ...

PENDLETON: (INTERRUPTING) Say... if I ain't bein' too irrelevant, is this the Maxhouse-Well Coffee Company????

YOUNG: It's Nat Pendleton!

(APPLAUSE)

PENDLETON: Gee ... thanks ... Hello, Mr. O'Keefe ... and Mr. Young. Gosh I'm certainly ignighted to be presented among all these extinguished looking people.

PARKER: Hello, Nat... remember me....?

PENDLETON: Oh ... sure... Miss Parker ... Say you'll have to excuse me for not noticin' your smiling countenance at first glance. I hope you'll accept my apologetics.

PARKER: (LAUGHING) Why certainly, Nat.

PENDLETON: Thanks, that's most ungracious of you. Bye the bye ... you sure look decapitating tonight. I ain't never seen you looking more elegant. (SHY LAUGH) Gosh ... you're pretty.

O'KEEFE: All right, Don Juan ... CUT!!!

YOUNG: Nat, you stepped right in the middle of a little round table discussion of "Burn 'Em Up O'Connor." Won't you — join in?

PENDLETON: "Burn 'Em Up O'Connor?" Who's he? A fireman?

O'KEEFE: Say, brain-wave ... don't tell me you've forgotten our picture already ... Remember ... automobile races ... crashes ... I'm driving a midget ...

PENDLETON: Well ... you oughta be ashamed to admit it ... a big fella like you pickin' on midgets ... it's obnoxious ... and as we say in French it's practically "Cherchez la femme."

O'KEEFE: (GROANS) Oh ……. You tell him, Cecilia …

PARKER: Look, Nat. Don't you remember Dennis playing the part of "Burn 'Em Up O'Connor?" Think now … You … Buddy Buttle his mechanic … the Indianapolis speedway … dizzy turns … burning cars … death-defying spills …

PENDLETON: (LAUGHS) Oh yeah, say I knew all the time the picture you was talkin' about. I was just makin' fun … ya know… tickling your invisibilities … (LAUGHS) I seen the picture at the preview.

O'KEEFE: What did you think of it, Nat?

PENDLETON: Do you want my unadulterated *candied* opinion?

O'KEEFE: No less.

PENDLETON: I liked it. I thought you and Miss Parker and everybody else was divine, but who was that dopey guy with the face like a pretzel that's supposed to be your helper?

O'KEEFE: Nat … that was YOU.

PENDLETON: It was? Me, personally?

O'KEEFE: There's no denyin' …

PENDLETON: You know … I KNEW I'd seen that face someplace before!

MORGAN: Oh, hello, everybody.

(THEY ALL GREET FRANK AD LIB)

MORGAN: Say, I saw that picture of yours — that Burn 'Em Up O'Connor — and I want to tell you I thought it was great.

PENDLETON: You liked it, huh?

MORGAN: Did I? Ah — it brought me back to the old days when I streaked the red track in Indianapolis, piloting my Stutz Bear Cat without —

YOUNG: Frank! Are you trying to tell these people you were a race driver, Mr. Morgan?

MORGAN: Dare-Devil Morgan, sir! The nerviest driver that ever skidded a car around a turn! I used to start every race by nailing my accelerator to the floor, and I always finished either in front or in the hospital.

O'KEEFE: When did you do your racing, Frank?

MORGAN: It was before your time, I should say, my boy.

YOUNG: Oh, you can count on that, Dennis!

MORGAN: My most spectacular exploit was probably in the race of 1912 against the greatest field of drivers that ever assembled on a track. I was driving a Morgan Special, and as luck would have it, I only managed to arrive at the track ten seconds before the race began. My car was standing in the pits — I looked around for my mechanic — he was nowhere to be found!

O'KEEFE: What did you do?

MORGAN: I looked around for the fellow — I couldn't wait, so I clapped on my helmet and started. Needless to say, I led the field for the first four hundred miles.

O'KEEFE: No motor trouble, in all that time?

MORGAN: It was astounding! I had my fingers crossed, I couldn't believe my good fortune — but when I had just five laps to go, fate caught up with me.

YOUNG: Fate? What was he driving?

MORGAN: Don't interrupt! The other drivers were right on my tail, bunched behind me, when suddenly I heard a terrific knocking in my motor. It was so heavy I feared the car would fall apart — but I kept on going —

O'KEEFE: Gee — and no mechanic to fix it!

MORGAN: That was the trouble! Tearing along at a hundred and ten miles an hour, I locked my ankle in the steering

	wheel and reached out over the hood with a wrench. I lifted it — and what do you think?
YOUNG:	What?
MORGAN:	My mechanic was in there, pounding with a hammer. So I put him in the rumble seat, and we won the race. Well, so long fellows!
YOUNG:	We can't do anything about him. But it was grand of all of you to drop in — and I know we're going to enjoy "Burn 'Em Up O'Connor."
	(APPLAUSE)
YOUNG:	Well — now Tony Martin again. Say, Tony — any word on the fifth race yet?
TONY:	No. We ought to get a flash in about twenty minutes, though, Bob.
YOUNG:	All right, you keep singing. This time, another oldie that's coming back to life — you all remember "I Cried For You."
	"I CRIED FOR YOU" —MARTIN AND ORCHESTRA
	(APPLAUSE)
YOUNG:	And now ladies and gentlemen, continuing our Maxwell House Program—
HANLEY:	Excuse me, Bob.
YOUNG:	Hello, Daddy. What's on your mind?
HANLEY:	I — er — I came to ask you a favor.
YOUNG:	Yes?
HANLEY:	You know that poem that Snooks recited a couple of weeks ago—
YOUNG:	The Owl and the Pussycat? Yes.

HANLEY: Well — she's been pestering me to let her — you know, the kid —

YOUNG: Mm-hmm. Stage-struck, huh?

HANLEY: (BRIDLING) What do you mean, stage-struck! She can recite as well as your kid!

YOUNG: All right, Daddy — don't lose your temper. We'll be very happy to let Snooks recite another poem. Bring her on!

HANLEY: Thanks ….. Oh, Snooks!

BRICE: Yes, daddy.

HANLEY: Go ahead and recite.

BRICE: Awrite …… Er—

HANLEY: Give the title. Go on.

BRICE: The THREE LITTLE KITTENS.

HANLEY: Fine. (BRICE RECITES "THE THREE LITTLE KITTENS" POEM)

YOUNG: Now here's Warren Hull with not one, but several words to the wise. Am I right, Warren?

HULL: Right as usual, Robert. (LAUGHS) For it's the wiser sex I'd like to talk to for just a moment.

Ladies, when you go to your grocer's tomorrow, just run your eye along the shelves where he keeps his coffee. When you come to those familiar blue cans you know contain Maxwell House Coffee, look a little more closely. You'll see that some of the cans of Maxwell House are plainly marked with the words — "drip grind." The others are labeled — "regular grind."

Now, of course, in *every* can of the *new* Maxwell House today, there's an extra richness, an extra full-bodied flavor and goodness that the wonderfully improved blend and new roasting process have made possible.

But there's a real reason why Maxwell House comes to

you in not one but two different grinds. If I asked you why, I'm pretty sure you'd say right away:

WOMAN'S VOICE(MATURE): (IN FAST) That's easy! I've learned from experience there's no such thing as a satisfactory all-purpose grind of coffee. To get the best results day in and day out, I know I *must* use coffee that comes correctly ground for the way I *make* it in my home.

HULL: Exactly! And because we *know* that's true ... because we want to help you enjoy the marvelous flavor and fragrance of this *new* Maxwell House to the fullest ... we've developed *two* scientifically correct grinds.

You'll find the *regular* grind Maxwell House comes just right for perfect results by percolator or boiled methods. Or, if you prefer drip coffee, the special *drip* grind will give you clear, sparkling full-flavored coffee in *any* type of drip or glass coffeemaker.

So ... try a pound of the *new* Maxwell House tomorrow. Or, if yours is a large family, you'll find the two-pound can economical and convenient.

And remember to ask for the grind that's right for *your* method of making coffee. You'll discover just one more reason why Maxwell House Coffee, famous for over half a century, is today giving pleasure to more people than ever before in its history!

(MUSIC BRIDGE)

YOUNG: Now — Miliza Korjus again. This time she's a guest in Meredith Willson's Concert Hall, and she sings a very beautiful arrangement of Rimsky Korsakoff's Immortal "Song of India." Miss Korjus —

"SONG OF INDIA" — KORJUS AND ORCH

(APPLAUSE)

"IF MEN WENT APARTMENT HUNTING AS WOMEN DO."
YOUNG - MORGAN - WILLSON - STAFFORD

HULL: Here is another of those Good News satires. This one is titled …. "IF MEN WENT APARTMENT HUNTING AS WOMEN DO." Bob Young and Hanley Stafford are trying to help Frank Morgan find a new apartment. Here they are, riding along in Morgan's car!

SOUND: (AUTOMOBILE)

MORGAN: Boys, this apartment hunting is wearing my nerves to a shallow fringe.

YOUNG: I'll say, and did you get a load of that horrible looking landlord at the last place? Ugh! What a face! I've seen better looking pans under an ice-box!

MORGAN: Stafford, what time is it?

STAFFORD: It must be five o'clock. I looked at my watch about an hour ago and it was two and I keep it an hour fast … so it MUST be five.

MORGAN: Well, I just have time to look at one more place and then I have to get home and start cooking dinner. What have we got checked off next in the want-ads …?

YOUNG: Let's see. Oh here …. Morgan … this sounds like a darling little place … listen: "For rent …. furnished apartment. Nice and airy …. sunshine right outside front door on Fourth Street — between Fifth and Sixth. The Venus Di Milo Arms."

MORGAN: The Venus Di Milo Arms? Sounds enchanting — let's go!

STAFFORD: Say, Morgan …. you still haven't told us why you're moving from the place where you live now. Denny O'Keefe said that it's a perfectly precious little apartment.

MORGAN:	Little is right … we were so cramped my poor little dog had to wag his tail up and down instead of sideways!!!
STAFFORD:	Say, I just adore your little dog. What is he, a Pekinese or a Great Dane?
MORGAN:	Oh, he's a very rare breed. He's a cross between an English Cur and a Scotch Mongrel! I'm going to enter him the dog show.
YOUNG:	Do you think he'll win?
MORGAN:	No…. but he'll meet some nice dogs!!!
SOUND:	(CAR NOISE UP….. FADES …. CAR COMES TO STOP)
MORGAN:	Well, here's the place and here's a wonderful place to park …. right in front of this fire hydrant.
YOUNG:	Morgan, you're the luckiest one when it comes to finding parking places.
MORGAN:	(GIGGLES) Alma used to say the same thing when she was courting me.
STAFFORD:	Looks like they should have some very sweet apartments in here … let's see … the sign says …. "Manager …. One flight up."
MORGAN:	Let's walk up … it'll do me good. I gained two pounds last week and I can hardly get into my volley-ball britches!!
MORGAN:	(AFTER SLIGHT PAUSE) Here … this door says "Manager"; I'll knock.
SOUND:	DOOR KNOCK.
WILLSON:	(OPENING DOOR) Well, what can I do for you gentle—
MORGAN:	Why Willson … What in heaven's name are you doing here?

"GOOD NEWS OF 1939" January 12, 1939   35

ALL:	Willson ….of all people …. well, get him …. etc:
WILLSON:	Come in, boys …. I'm the manager here … I get my rent cheaper that way. Won't you all sit down and make yourselves "ta-hum?" (PROP LAUGH) How about something to drink???
ALL:	Good …. wonderful …. I'm famished … etc:
WILLSON:	What'll you have, Young?
YOUNG:	A coke.
WILLSON:	Staffy-boy?
STAFFORD:	I'll take orange juice.
WILLSON:	MORGAN?
MORGAN:	Just plain water for me … You see …. I'M DRIVING!!!!
WILLSON:	Well, boys … here you are. I have it right handy here. My but you're all looking simply stunning … and Stafford, you've *done* something to your hair.
STAFFORD:	I was waiting for you to notice it. How do you like it?
WILLSON:	It's positively exotic … that's what it is … exotic!!!!
STAFFORD:	It's so simple, too. I just let my sideburns grow and hennaed one and bleached the other one.
MORGAN:	I did the same thing with my car. Had half of it painted red and the other half painted blue.
YOUNG:	I meant to ask you about that, Morgan … it looks very peculiar.
MORGAN:	I know … but every time I have an accident … you should hear the witnesses contradict each other … (GIGGLES)
STAFFORD:	Say, Morgan, we better get a look at that apartment, I just must get home. I have an Orange-Meringue-Broccoli-Dream cake in the oven …

WILLSON: Well, this is the apartment that's for rent — how do you like it?

MORGAN: How many rooms?

WILLSON: Six rooms — parlor — bath — kitchen and 3 closets!!

STAFFORD: It's rather dark, isn't it?

WILLSON: Well … it's usually sunny… but the woman next door had twins last week and her clothes-line runs right by this window.

YOUNG: It seems to be a nice quiet place, anyway.

WILLSON: Oh yes… we don't allow any pets, children, radios or phonographs….

MORGAN: Do you think they'd mind much? I have a fountain pen that scratches just a little?

YOUNG: You don't allow children? How about the twins next door?

WILLSON: Well, they didn't have them when they moved in. It just goes to show you, you can't trust a tenant!!

STAFFORD: Have you a refrigerator here…???

WILLSON: No… but we have a perfectly adorable ice-woman and she comes in SO handy if you ever need a fourth at bridge.

MORGAN: Is this the only apartment in the building for rent…???

WILLSON: No, there's one right across the hall. It's a studio apartment. The door is unlocked. Just open it and take three steps down. The light is on your left.

MORGAN: (FADING) I'll be right back, boys…

YOUNG: What's this, Willson?

WILLSON: That's the wall-bed. Oh, oh… don't pull it down… my father is asleep there!!!

YOUNG: I'm sorry …

WILLSON: That's the bathroom-door there, Stafford…

STAFFORD: I'll just peek in… (OPENS DOOR) OH… EXCUSE ME! (SHUTS IT) Willson, there's somebody taking a bath in there!!!

WILLSON: Oh, that's my brother Cedric…

STAFFORD: My, isn't he skinny???

MORGAN: (OFF MIKE) (TERRIFYING SCREAM…)

ALL: That's Morgan!! What happened to him….???? Morgan… Where are you….????

WILLSON: Boys…. look!!!! Morgan opened the wrong door and fell down the elevator shaft!!!!

YOUNG: (CALLS DOWN) MORGAN!!! MORGAN!! ARE YOU ALL RIGHT…??

MORGAN: Yes… of course… but Hey… if you're coming down to look at this apartment… watch out for that first step… it's a honey…!!!

(MUSIC UP … APPLAUSE)

YOUNG: Well, ladies and gentlemen — next week we're going to have another great show — with a special return engagement of the two stars you enjoyed so much last Thursday — with Melvyn Douglas and Virginia Bruce. Another welcome guest will be the famous Russian soprano, Zarova — and of course you'll want to hear Fanny Brice and Hanley Stafford, Frank Morgan, Tony Martin, and Meredith Willson. In the meantime —

HULL: Say, Bob —

YOUNG: Yes, Warren.

HULL: I just got the results of the fifth race.

WILLSON: Huh? Did Blue Bolt get it?

MARTIN: Was it Green Goddess?

YOUNG: What about White Queen? That's what Morgan gave me.

HULL: Yes — and he gave me Yellow Jack.

WILLSON: Well, who won it?

HULL: A horse called Color Blind — won by eight lengths!

MORGAN: Warren! Did you say Color Blind?

HULL: Yes.

MORGAN: I had it! So long, fellows!

YOUNG: Good old Frank! Well, see you next week, ladies and gentlemen — and in the meantime, go to the movies and take the family with you. I want to give my personal endorsement to one great picture — the world famous production of George Bernard Shaw's "Pygmalion," with Leslie Howard and the new discovery Wendy Hiller, opening at the Loew's Theatre in Dayton, Ohio — on Thursday, January 19th. Don't miss it! This is Bob Young, saying goodnight until next Thursday.

(MUSIC UP)

HULL: This is Warren Hull saying Goodnight and Good Luck for Maxwell House — the coffee that's always good to the last drop.

This is the National Broadcasting Company.

MAXWELL HOUSE
Presents
"GOOD NEWS OF 1939"
January 26, 1939
#57

CAST

1. Warren Hull
2. Robert Young
3. Lionel Barrymore
4. Mickey Rooney
5. Douglas McPhail
6. Zarova
7. Frank Morgan
8. Fanny Brice
9. Hanley Stafford
10. Meredith Willson and Orchestra
11. Max Terr Chorus

1.	(OPENING) ("RISE 'N' SHINE" — BAND)
2.	"GIVE A MAN A HORSE HE CAN RIDE" —MCPHAIL
3-3H.	BABY SNOOKS
4-4A.	COMMERCIAL
5.	"HOW STRANGE" —BAND - ZAROVA
6-6F.	MORGAN - YOUNG
7.	STATION BREAK
8.	"JEEPERS CREEPERS" —BAND
9-9P.	DRAMA: "A BARGAIN WITH LINCOLN" —BARRYMORE - ROONEY

10.	CONCERT HALL — QUARTET: "WAY DOWN YONDER IN THE CORNFIELDS" — MORGAN - YOUNG - WILLSON - HULL
11-11A.	COMMERCIAL
12.	CONCERT HALL: "ON THE ROAD TO MANDALAY" — MCPHAIL
13-13A.	"HAPPY LITTLE FARMER" — ENTIRE COMPANY
14.	CLOSING

HULL: Maxwell House Coffee presents ... Good News of 1939!

(MUSIC IN AND FADE)

HULL: The makers of Maxwell House Coffee welcome you to another hour of entertainment from Metro-Goldwyn-Mayer Studios in Hollywood, with the regular Good News cast of entertainers, Fanny Brice and Hanley Stafford, Frank Morgan, Douglas McPhail and Meredith Willson — plus two distinguished guests of honor you will hear about in a moment. Meredith Willson starts the program with "Rise 'n' Shine!"

"RISE 'N' SHINE" — MEREDITH WILLSON & ORCHESTRA

(APPLAUSE)

HULL: Now here is your host for the evening — Robert Young!

YOUNG: Thank you, Warren. We haven't really got much chance of surprising the subscribers with tonight's guests, because both of them were with us at the finish of last week's program and promised to be here today. Well — they're here, and I know you'll enjoy their performances — Mister Lionel Barrymore and Master Mickey Rooney!

(APPLAUSE)

BARRYMORE:	Thank you. Er — Bob, don't you think Mickey's getting old enough now so he could be called Mister?
MICKEY:	Gee, thanks, Mr. Barrymore!
BARRYMORE:	That's all right.
YOUNG:	I stand corrected. Our guests of honor are Mr. Lionel Barrymore and Mr. — Michael — Rooney. (MICKEY SKULLS IT) And now that we've got this important problem in etiquette cleared up, we're going to hear from Douglas McPhail. How are you tonight, Doug?
MCPHAIL:	Fine, thanks, Bob.
YOUNG:	Doug, as a favor to me, I wish you'd tell the audience how you happened to pick the song you're going to sing for us now.
MCPHAIL:	Well, Bob, you know I've always admired Nelson Eddy, and several years ago I heard him sing this number in a concert. And I got such a kick out of it that I always wanted to sing it myself. And — well, that's it, I guess.
YOUNG:	Yes — all but the name of the song. Ladies and gentlemen, Douglas McPhail sings "Give a Man a Horse He Can Ride."
	"GIVE A MAN A HORSE HE CAN RIDE" — MCPHAIL AND ORCHESTRA
SOUND:	(CLOP CLOP)
YOUNG:	Thanks, Doug! And stick around! Now, ladies and gentlemen, here is Fanny Brice as Baby Snooks!
	(MUSIC ... APPLAUSE)
YOUNG:	Daddy, played by Hanley Stafford, is not home from the office yet, and Snooks is going to take care of her baby brother in the nursery while Mother prepares to go to the store. Here they are.
MOTHER:	Now, Snooks, I want you to play nicely with the baby.

BRICE: Awight, Mummy. Come here, little sweetheart.

MOTHER: I'll be back in fifteen minutes.

BRICE: Waahhhh!

MOTHER: What's the matter?

BRICE: He pulled my hair!

MOTHER: Never mind, Snooks. Don't get angry — the baby doesn't know how it hurts.

BRICE: Don't he?

MOTHER: No. Play nicely — I'm going now.

SOUND: (BABY HOWLS)

BRICE: (LAUGHS)

MOTHER: Snooks! What's the matter with the baby?

BRICE: He knows how it hurts now, Mummy!

MOTHER: That's terrible! Why don't you play a nice game with him?

BRICE: Awight. We'll play automobile.

MOTHER: All right. I'll be right back.

SOUND: (BABY HOWLS)

MOTHER: Snooks! I thought you said you were going to play automobile with the baby!

BRICE: I am, Mummy.

MOTHER: Then why did you pinch him and make him yell?

BRICE: He's the horn!

MOTHER: Oh, well! I can see I'll have to take the baby to the store with me.

BRICE: What shall I do, Mummy?

MOTHER:	You stay here and play with your blocks. Daddy'll be home in a few minutes.
BRICE:	What's this, Mummy?
MOTHER:	That's my lip rouge — give it to me.
BRICE:	I'm gonna paint my face and play Indian!
MOTHER:	Snooks! Stop making those spots on your face — that stuff's hard to get off! Give me that rouge.
BRICE:	(LAUGHS) Do I look funny?
MOTHER:	Go wash the rouge off! I'll be back soon. Goodbye.
SOUND:	(DOOR SLAM)
BRICE:	(SINGS) Sally go round the stars — Sally go round the moon — Sally go round the chimney pots every afternoon!
SOUND:	(DOOR OPENS AND CLOSES)
FATHER:	(TIRED) Hello, Snooks!
BRICE:	(BRIGHT) Hello, Daddy!
FATHER:	Get my slippers, Snooks. I'm completely worn out.
BRICE:	Why?
FATHER:	Because I've been working very hard. Hurry up and get — Snooks!
BRICE:	Huh?
FATHER:	(ALARMED) What's that on your face?
BRICE:	What?
FATHER:	Those red spots! Get in bed, quick. Here — stick this thermometer in your mouth … Good heavens! My poor child!
BRICE:	Am I sick, Daddy?

FATHER: Let me call the doctor … (OVER DIALING) We'll have you well soon, darling. Hello … Doc? This is Higgins. I'm afraid Snooks has the measles!

BRICE: (LAUGHS) WAAAHHH!

FATHER: Quiet, honey — don't be scared. Hello … her temperature? Just a minute … what does the thermometer say, Snooks?

BRICE: I didn't hear nothing, Daddy.

FATHER: No — the number! What number does it say?

BRICE: Um — er — hundred and fifty-four.

FATHER: Hello — hundred and fifty-four! Huh? Wait a minute — Snooks, let me see that thermometer. Hello, Doc — I can't read it very well — my hands are shaking. Yes — and she has red spots on her face …

BRICE: Daddy!

FATHER: Don't talk, Snooks. Hello … Yes — yes. And give her a dose of — of what? Spell it, Doc … (SPELLS LIKE REPEATING) P-A-R-E-G-O-R-I-C …

BRICE: WAAAAHHH!

FATHER: What's the matter, Snooks?

BRICE: I don't want no castor oil!

FATHER: This is not castor oil.

BRICE: Then why you spelling it?

FATHER: Please, darling — don't get excited. Hello, Doc … Yes? (A WRECK) No — I'm not nervous … I can handle it — but you'd better hurry over here. All right … yes — I'll make her take it. Goodbye. Ohhh!

BRICE: Are you sick, Daddy?

FATHER: No — but you are, my child. I may have to get somebody to watch you.

BRICE:	Who?
FATHER:	I — I'll get you a trained nurse.
BRICE:	Will she do tricks?
FATHER:	No, dear. Sit up a minute, Snooks. I want to have a look at your throat. Open your mouth … wider …
BRICE:	Ahhhhhhh!
FATHER:	Hmm — looks a little angry.
BRICE:	Who's it mad at, Daddy?
FATHER:	No — I mean it's inflamed. I may have to paint it.
BRICE:	Why?
FATHER:	Because I think you have acute tonsillitis.
BRICE:	You like it, Daddy?
FATHER:	Now, listen, Snooks. I want you to take one of these pills.
BRICE:	I don't wanna.
FATHER:	Please, dear. They won't hurt you. Look — if you take one I'll take one, too.
BRICE:	Awight. Take yours first.
FATHER:	All right — watch … (SWALLOWS) There! I've swallowed it.
BRICE:	Waaaah!
FATHER:	What's the matter?
BRICE:	That's the one I wanted!
FATHER:	Well, listen — will you take some medicine then?
BRICE:	No!
FATHER:	Oh, Snooks. You must take it, otherwise you'll never get well.

BRICE: I ain't sick.

FATHER: Yes you are. You've got the measles.

BRICE: Why?

FATHER: Because you have those red spots on your face.

BRICE: Ohhh … Daddy?

FATHER: Yes?

BRICE: Can I stay home from school if those red spots ain't the measles?

FATHER: Of course not!

BRICE: (QUICKLY) It's the measles!

FATHER: I know it is! Don't you think I know enough about medicine! I recognized it instantly!

BRICE: What makes measles, Daddy?

FATHER: It's caused by a little germ.

BRICE: A German?

FATHER: No — a germ.

BRICE: What's a germ?

FATHER: It's a tiny little animal that causes plenty of trouble.

BRICE: My doggie's got germs on it.

FATHER: How do you know?

BRICE: I seen one hop!

FATHER: Nonsense. You can't see germs — only under the microscope. Now, here — I've got some medicine in this spoon. I want you to swallow it.

BRICE: I don't want it. It tastes bad.

FATHER: Please, Snooks — it's delicious — it's wonderful — it tastes beautiful.

BRICE:	You like it, Daddy?
FATHER:	Oh, I love it!
BRICE:	Awight.
FATHER:	That's a good girl! Now — careful — hold your mouth open — careful —
BRICE:	Waaahhh!
FATHER:	Snooks! You've spilled it all over the bed!
BRICE:	I don't like it!
FATHER:	Oh, what am I going to do with you?
BRICE:	Kiss me, Daddy!
FATHER:	No — no! Snooks — please! Don't kiss me!
BRICE:	Why?
FATHER:	Well — I — I might catch the measles! That's how it spreads.
BRICE:	I wanna kiss you!
FATHER:	Snooks! Don't jump on me —
BRICE:	Wheeeee!
FATHER:	Snooks! Please — (MUFFLED STRUGGLES) — Oh! You kissed me!
BRICE:	Are you sick, Daddy?
FATHER:	I don't know — I didn't feel too good when I came in … You shouldn't have —
BRICE:	Daddy?
FATHER:	What is it?
BRICE:	You got a red spot on your face.
FATHER:	Huh? Where? Let me look in the mirror … Ohhhhh! It's there! What shall I do?

BRICE:	Take some more medicine, Daddy!
FATHER:	Ohhh! I feel terrible! I'm groggy! I didn't know it worked so fast. Move over, Snooks.
BRICE:	What's the matter?
FATHER:	I wanna lie down. Where's that broken-down doctor? Why doesn't he hurry! Ohhhh — I'm terribly ill!
BRICE:	I'm sowwy, Daddy.
FATHER:	(HE MEANS IT) Oh, Snooks, dear — if I ever live through this I'll — I'll never lift my hand in anger to you again. Now I repent ever having spanked you — I promise I'll never hit you again!
BRICE:	(PLEASED) You ain't never gonna spank me no more, Daddy?
FATHER:	Never! Life is too short! Ohhh — am I sick.
SOUND:	(DOOR SLAM)
BRICE:	Hello, Mummy!
MOTHER:	Hello. What's the matter here?
FATHER:	Oh, Mother — I'm dying, I caught the measles from Snooks.
MOTHER:	Measles! Why, you big baby! That's lip rouge!
FATHER:	(SUDDENLY ALIVE) Huh? LIP ROUGE!
BRICE:	I think I better go now!
FATHER:	Come here, you! Why didn't you tell me it was lip rouge?
BRICE:	You didn't ask me! Daddy — you promised me —
FATHER:	I'll promise you! (WHACK)
BRICE:	WAAAHHHH!
	(MUSIC ... APPLAUSE)

HULL:	Bob, may I have the stage for a moment?
YOUNG:	The stage is yours, Warren ... the widest stage and the largest audience in the whole wide world.
HULL:	The time is breakfast this morning. The place — any home up the street. Let's listen ...
SOUND:	(FADE IN CLOCK TICKING AND HOLD UNDER DIALOGUE)
HUSBAND:	Well, see you tonight, Mary. I've gotta run.
WIFE:	But, Bill. It's only a quarter after. And you've only half-finished your coffee again this morning. Don't you like ...
HUSBAND:	(ABRUPTLY) It's all right. So long, dear. (START FADING) Home the usual time ...
HULL:	Has anything like that happened in *your* home?
	You see, for most men coffee makes the meal. And if you've noticed any half-finished cups of coffee on *your* table lately, we'd like to suggest just this — try serving the *new* Maxwell House.
	Today, this famous blend of superb coffee is wonderfully richer, more delicious, with a downright satisfying flavor your husband's just bound to enjoy. And to bring you the true, natural goodness of these marvelous coffees at their best, we've developed the amazing "radiant roast" process, which roasts each coffee bean evenly *all the way through*. Then, to make sure you get the most from your Maxwell House in the *making* we offer it to you in two scientifically correct grinds. There's regular grind Maxwell House, for perfect results by percolator or boiled methods, or the special drip grind, for clear, sparkling, full-flavored coffee in *any* type of drip of glass coffeemaker.
	Why not treat yourself and your husband to a pound of the *new* Maxwell House tomorrow? Or, if yours is a large family, you'll find the two-pound can economical

	and convenient. You'll discover for yourself why more people are buying Maxwell House Coffee today than ever before in its history.
	(MUSIC BRIDGE)
YOUNG:	Now a charming young lady who has visited our good news program before — Miss Zarova, with Meredith Willson and the Maxwell House Chorus, present a russian song from the new norma shearer-clark gable picture, "Idiot's Delight" — "How Strange."
	"HOW STRANGE" —ZAROVA, CHORUS & ORCHESTRA
	(APPLAUSE)
YOUNG:	That was beautiful, Madame!
ZAROVA:	Thank you, Mr. Young.
MORGAN:	Oh! Oatken koroso, moya krah-sah-veetsa. Oatken korosko.
ZAROVA:	Spasivo, spasivo, Maestro!
MORGAN:	Coat ketya gooliat sam noy, Madame?
ZAROVA:	Oh da da! Dad a!
MORGAN:	Ma ma — ma ma!
YOUNG:	(WHISTLES)
MORGAN:	Ya za yaydoo za vami say vodnya veherom!
ZAROVA:	(ANSWERS HIM AND GOES OUT)
MORGAN:	Ah. Bublichki va droshky sev noy!
YOUNG:	What is this, Frank?
MORGAN:	Nothing. I hope she's there tonight!
YOUNG:	Frank, why do you put on such an act? Who are you trying to impress with that Russian stuff?

MORGAN: Whom.

YOUNG: All right, whom. I doubt if you were talking Russian at all, and if you were, it's something you got out of a guidebook.

MORGAN: My dear friend — or possibly I should say — Tovarich — the happiest years of my life were spent in Russia — sleighing through the streets of Moscow, strolling through the squares of Nijni-Novgorod, slipping on the steppes of Siberia — Ah, Russia, my heart is in thy frozen peaks, my soul cries out for —

YOUNG: Frank! You can prove all this, can't you?

MORGAN: Of course, Tovarich!

YOUNG: That's fine. Meredith, I want to borrow your first violinist.

MEREDITH: Sure.

YOUNG: (CALLS) Leon! Come over here, will you? Frank, here's a member of Meredith's orchestra that used to play fiddle for the Czar. Leon, shake hands with Frank Morgan.

MORGAN: How do you do?

YOUNG: Now, I'd like to hear you two Tovariches have a little conversation.

MORGAN: (LOOKS AT WATCH) Well, I haven't much time, I —

LEON: (RUSSIAN SPEECH)

YOUNG: I suppose you understand every word he said, Frank?

MORGAN: Er — no. The fellow speaks with a heavy Ukranian brogue. I've got to be going, Bob, I —

YOUNG: Wait a minute! Thanks, Leon. (LEON BLOWS) Frank, I just wanted you to admit you were faking.

MORGAN: Well, to tell you the truth, Bob, I didn't spend a great deal of time in Russia. I was just — er — passing through on my way to — er — Sweden.

YOUNG: Sweden?

MORGAN: Sweden, yes.

YOUNG: I see. (CALLS) Say — OLEE!

MORGAN: (QUICKLY) Er — did I go through Sweden fast! (GIGGLES)

YOUNG: Uh-huh. You just passed through Sweden on your way to — er?

MORGAN: Er — I passed through Sweden on my way to China.

YOUNG: Oh, the shortcut.

MORGAN: The scenic route. You know, Bob, there's something fascinating about the Orient. When I was in China, I —

YOUNG: Yes. (CALLS) Say — Ling Foo!

MORGAN: I've been stabbed! He's got a Chinese piccolo player!

YOUNG: Well, I guess that cleans up Morgan the Traveler. You haven't been to Russia, you haven't been to Sweden, and you haven't been to China.

MORGAN: (MUMBLES) Russia — Sweden — China — er — Meredith! You haven't any Hindus in your orchestra, have you?

MEREDITH: No, Frank.

MORGAN: There's a country! (GIGGLES) Ah, India! My heart is in thy frozen peaks — my soul cries out for another glimpse of the fountains of the Taj Mahal, the jeweled temples of Hyderabad … India! I can see it all in the crystal ball of my mind. Once again, through the mysterious hanging gardens of Delhi, I walk, bare-footed. At sunset, before the secret idol in the lamasery at Simla, I bow. Once

	again, by the rush-covered banks of the sacred, surging Ganges, I lie.
YOUNG:	You lie.
MORGAN:	Yes. Oh, well! (HE MUMBLES SOMETHING TO HIMSELF, SORE) I guess I don't have to stay around and take this — who do these fellows think —
MEREDITH:	Don't go, Frank! Wait a minute!
MORGAN:	(KEEPS MUMBLING)
YOUNG:	Aw, I was only kidding, Frank!
MEREDITH:	Tell us some more! I love it!
MORGAN:	(VERY BRIGHT) You really want to hear it?
YOUNG & MEREDITH:	Sure!
MORGAN:	Well, it was several years before the War, and I was stationed at Bombay, a dashing young subaltern in the Royal Bengal Lancers, a servant of her majesty the Queen.
YOUNG:	And of all the black-faced crew, the finest man I knew.
MORGAN:	Was the regimental beastie, Gunga Din! It was Din, Din, D — what the — that's the last straw, Young!
MEREDITH:	(MAD) Leave him alone, Bob! This is interesting! Go on, Frank!
MORGAN:	Thank you, Meredith. I was stationed in the plains behind Calcutta my first summer out there, and the heat was unbearable. A young soldier could scarcely have had a more disagreeable initiation into Indian life — but I managed to keep fit through the services of a native masseur.
YOUNG:	India rubber. Imagine it, Meredith.
MEREDITH:	Yes.

MORGAN: Day after day, week after week, month after month, strange India faces around me, hours of drudgery and routine duty — but I attacked it with relish!

YOUNG: India relish.

MORGAN: Young, you tell worse jokes every week — but today you sound like the week after next!

MEREDITH: Cut it out, Bob! A thousand pardons, Sahib!

MORGAN: Meredith, I've never appreciated you enough. You're an excellent fellow — in a distasteful sort of way. I must remember to send you a bottle of Diedesheimer, 1926 — I think you'd like it.

MEREDITH: Gee, thank you, Sahib!

YOUNG: Thank him when you get it, Meredith. Go ahead with the story, Howdah!

MORGAN: Yes. The worst problem that first year was the constant battle against the dreaded scourge of the lowlands —The Fever.

YOUNG: How did you fight it, Frank?

MORGAN: I had a special anti-fever diet, aspirin and whiskey, half and half.

YOUNG: What do you mean, half and half?

MORGAN: Half an aspirin, half a quart of whiskey. (I certainly got tired of the aspirin.) Ah me! Well, all this happened in the lowlands, of course. But you know the best place to be during the Indian fever season!

YOUNG: Pasadena.

MORGAN: No, the hills! There's no fever in the hills, but even there it's a constant fight for existence! The natives in the hill country tremble at the mere mention of that jungle menace —Simba!

YOUNG: Lion!

MEREDITH: He is not! ... Tell us about Simba, Frank!

MORGAN: Well — Simba is the native word for killer lion, Meredith.

MEREDITH: Oh. Pardon, Bob.

MORGAN: Our regiment went to the hills when the rains began —and we found the natives in a terrific state of excitement!

MEREDITH: Simba!

MORGAN: Yes! But this time they had good reason! An enormous lion had gone Coomla, as the natives say. It means crazy.

YOUNG: Was he attacking humans?

MORGAN: It was ghastly! Not a day passed but what Simba descended on a native village and carried off some hapless human prey to devour in the jungle! He decimated the population of the entire district, and became bolder with each raid. The natives were in terror, but the regiment was soon to hear from Simba, too!

YOUNG: You mean to say he came right into your camp?

MORGAN: Worse than that! One afternoon about four o'clock I was playing bridge in the officers' mess. Major Athol, on my left, had just bid seven spades, and he was about to play the hand, when, quicker than I can tell it, a huge yellow body flashed across the table, seized the major, and whisked him out into the jungle! I didn't hesitate an instant!

MEREDITH: What did you do?

MORGAN: I looked at the Major's cards; he couldn't have made it anyway. But Simba's insolence had gone too far.

YOUNG: Why didn't you shoot him on the spot?

MORGAN: My dear boy, when Simba is Coomla, he is sacred. If we'd killed him there'd have been a native uprising at

	once. So I determined to catch him alive. It would make me an immortal in regimental history. That very night I set out through the jungle, alone except for a hundred native beaters and five gun bearers. It was terrifying — a thousand jungle noises, green eyes glaring at us out of the darkness — and suddenly we heard a thunderous crashing in the underbrush, and a flock of mastodons went rushing past us, not a hundred feet away!
YOUNG:	I thought the mastodons were extinct.
MORGAN:	They do, but the wind was the other way. We continued hacking our way through the brush, until one of the beaters came running back to me, his eyes filled with terror. "Sahib. Simba gajput!" he exclaimed. He had discovered the spoor!
MEREDITH:	You got him now, Frank!
MORGAN:	Not yet! It was only by an iron will that I controlled the nervousness of my beaters, and forced them to dig a pit across the lion's trail to the waterhole. Forty feet deep, twenty feet across, they dug, while I patiently smoked a cheroot.
YOUNG:	What a job!
MORGAN:	When the pit was finished, we covered it with branches and dead leaves, 'til it was smooth as the rest of the jungle floor. Then we gathered our tools, and since we knew Simba would not feed before morning, we returned to camp, and retired for the night.
MEREDITH:	Gee, this is interesting!
MORGAN:	At five o'clock in the morning the entire camp was aroused by the most hideous screeching and howling. The whole regiment turned out at once, and the native beaters led the way to the pit. The General himself, with drawn pistol, advanced to the edge of the trap, and parted the branches. Imagine my feelings as he looked down at the helpless raging creature within!

YOUNG: It was Simba!

MORGAN: No, it was me. I must have been walking in my sleep. Well, so long, fellows, I'll see you later!

(MUSIC ... APPLAUSE)

COMMERCIAL STATION BREAK

YOUNG: And now, there's the marvelous fragrance of freshly-made coffee in the air. It's time for our familiar Thursday evening custom ... a moment of relaxation over a steaming, friendly cup of the new Maxwell House Coffee.

BARRYMORE: Say, Bob ...

YOUNG: Mr. Barrymore ...

BARRYMORE: Bob, I'd just like to say that a good cup of coffee is mighty important to me. So I think this custom of yours is just fine. And if you wouldn't mind pouring out an extra cup ...

YOUNG: Mind? We'd be delighted, Mr. Barrymore. We're inviting you right now to join us and our friends all over the country in a cup of this coffee that's good to the last drop.

Warren, will you do the honors? And Meredith, strike up the band.

(MUSIC UP AND FADE FOR STATION ANNOUNCEMENT)

HULL: We now pause briefly for station identification.

(MUSIC UP AND FADE)

YOUNG: This is Bob Young again, and we continue our Maxwell House Good News program, guest-starring Lionel Barrymore and Mickey Rooney. Meredith Willson opens our second act with the best of the NEW fasties — Harry Warren's smash hit, "Jeepers Creepers."

"JEEPERS CREEPERS" —MEREDITH WILLSON & ORCHESTRA

(APPLAUSE)

YOUNG: Very good, Meredith — and very fast. Incidentally Harry Warren's going to visit our program next week. Now ladies and gentlemen, our MGM Theater of the Air production, starring Lionel Barrymore and Mickey Rooney. We present a short drama adapted especially for this occasion by Sidney Cook and Hartman Renaud, from a story by T. Morris Longstreth. It is called "A Bargain with Lincoln."

(MUSIC IN)

YOUNG: (OVER MUSIC) The time — the year 1863. Lincoln is in the White House, the War between the States is still raging. The scene — the kitchen of a farmhouse some ten miles outside of Washington. A middle-aged woman is tensely preparing supper.

(DRAMA SKETCH)

AFTER DRAMA - QUARTET

BARRYMORE: This is Lionel Barrymore, ladies and gentlemen. I'm not playing Lincoln now, but it's my duty to inform you that the stage here has been temporarily vacated by the Messieurs Young, Morgan, Hull, and Willson. They will shortly entertain you with a barbershop harmony quartet.

ROONEY: Why didn't they let us in on it, Mr. Barrymore?

BARRYMORE: Well, Mickey, I asked about that, and I was told they didn't have enough costumes.

ROONEY: It's a production!

BARRYMORE: So I gather. Here they come now! (BARRYMORE TALKS OVER THE LAUGHTER — QUARTET ENTERS) Ladies and gentlemen, the quartet is attired in the fashion of the Nineties, with striped peg-top trousers, high collars, straw hats, and canes. Now, if they could ONLY sing!

MORGAN: I resent that, Lionel!

BARRYMORE: Well, Frank, the burden of proof is on you — go ahead.

MEREDITH: (TO HIS COLLEAGUES) All right, boys, and Frank, try to remember not to follow Warren when he takes that high B.

MORGAN: Don't worry about me, Willson — you raven!

"WAY DOWN YONDER IN THE CORNFIELD"
—QUARTET

(APPLAUSE)

YOUNG: Friends, the other day I received this letter from Mrs. H. J. Ringler of Cuyohoga Falls, Ohio. Her letter is so interesting and sincere, that I want you to hear it.

WOMAN: Dear Mr. Young — I've listened to Good News now for more than a year. And I just have to acknowledge the pleasure your program and Maxwell House Coffee give my family.

First, let me tell you, I'm a *new* user of Maxwell House. For five years after I was married, my husband and myself carried on an extensive search for the right kind of coffee. As I was an economical housewife, I used the coffee after it was once purchased, regardless of quality. We began to believe that we were searching for the mythic gold at the end of the rainbow until one happy day when we first began using Maxwell House Coffee. That first breakfast, we knew that we had discovered something — a coffee whose richness and mellow flavor convinced us that it was the finest coffee ever. Maxwell House Coffee has now become a permanent member of our family.

HULL: Thank you, Mrs. Ringler. We really appreciate your fine letter.

Friends, people everywhere are turning to the *new* Maxwell House. That's because *today* that famous blend of superb coffee originated by Joel Cheek more than fifty years ago, is richer, more delicious, more full-bodies than ever before. You'll notice the difference in your very first cup. And to make sure you get the *true* natural coffee flavor of this wonderfully improved blend, Maxwell House is now roasted by the amazing new radiant roast process which roasts each coffee bean evenly *all the way through*. With radiant roast there's no longer any chance of bitter coffee due to parching — or weak coffee due to under-roasting. Your new Maxwell House is always full-bodied. Always smooth and mellow.

So if you haven't tried the *new* Maxwell House lately, get a pound and serve it to your family tomorrow. It comes in the same familiar blue super-vacuum can you've always known.

We think you'll agree with the millions who say — this new Maxwell House is more than ever — good to the last drop.

(MUSIC BRIDGE)

YOUNG: Well, now we're back in modern dress again, we can continue with Meredith Willson's concert hall presentation, which will be on a much higher musical plane than our last number. I think I can say that without fear of contradiction. Tonight, Meredith presents a number chosen by Mr. Michael Rooney, who continues the Kipling flavor of our program by selecting as the number which he would choose above all others to hear and preserve if all the music in the world had been destroyed — Douglas McPhail will sing it for us.

"ROAD TO MANDALAY" (RANGOON - BURMESE FOR APPLAUSE) —MCPHAIL AND ORCHESTRA

"HAPPY LITTLE FARMER"

YOUNG: Well, it seems that you folks have kinda taken to our little "Family Group Singing Bees" that we've been closing our programs with of late, so here's another weighty question I'm going to ask the great minds around here — Gather 'round, everybody. (MUSIC IN) In the winter what becomes of all the fields of hay?

ALL: We don't know ...

YOUNG: In the Winter magic they all seem to melt away ...

ALL: That's right ...

YOUNG: Well, what becomes of the Farmer in the Dell?

ALL: We don't know ...

YOUNG: Just gather in a little closer and Ole Doc Young will tell ...
Happy Little Farmer ... riding in a one horse open sleigh
Giddy ap Giddy ap Giddy ap
it's time for play.
When a Little Farmer ... puts away his one horse shay
Giddy ap Giddy ap Giddy ap
it's time for play.
When the ground is covered with snow
And the green things refuse to grow
I get out my toboggan and I hitch up Dobbin and way through the fields I go.
Happy Little Farmer ... Riding in a one horse sleigh ...
Giddy ap Giddy ap .. Giddy ap
It's time for play.

MORGAN: Happy Little Morgan ... Riding with a girl by my side ... Giddy ap giddy ap ... I'm satisfied ...

ROONEY: Happy Little Rooney ... I love to dance and sing ... Jig it up, Jig it up, Jig it up ... Come on, let's swing.

YOUNG: Mr. Barrymore …

BARRYMORE: When you find that you're feeling low
Days are dull and nights are slow
If you just wear a smile things will all be worthwhile
And away your cares will go …

MEREDITH: Happy Little Dithy (PROP LAUGH)(MUSIC SLOWS DOWN)
Boys the music's getting slow
Pick it up, pick it up, pick it up
That's it … Let's go!

SNOOKS: Happy Little Snooksy playing "Horsey" with Daddy all the day
Giddy ap Giddy ap Giddy ap (LAUGHS)
Faster, Daddy … I like to play

DADDY: (AS IF IT'S KILLING HIM) Happy little Daddy .. Oh yeah
Answers questions 'til it hurts …
Why, Daddy … Why, Daddy … Why, Daddy …
'Til I go nerts.

MCPHAIL: When it seems I just can't get along
Everything I try comes out wrong
I start humming a tune and I find pretty soon
Troubles go on the wings of a song …

HULL: Happy little Hull .. Talks Maxwell House all day
Drink it up … drink it up … drink it up
"It's great," you'll say …

CHORUS: (BACK TO MIDDLE STRAIN)
(UP TO ALL JOIN IN)
Giddy ap … Giddy ap … Giddy ap … It's time for play!

YOUNG: Mickey Rooney, could I have a word with you please?

ROONEY: I ain't done nothing!

YOUNG: You've been great, Mickey — I've got an invitation for you.

ROONEY: Yeah?

YOUNG: I was talking to Joe Mankiewicz yesterday — your producer on Huckleberry Finn — and he tells me the picture is all set and ready to go.

ROONEY: Uh-huh.

YOUNG: How'd you like to come on the program next week and give us a preview of the picture?

ROONEY: It's fine with me if it's okay with Mr. Mankiewicz.

YOUNG: Then it's a date for next Thursday. So long, Mickey and thanks!

ROONEY: So long!

YOUNG: Well, the rest of us will all be here, too — Fanny Brice and Hanley Stafford, Frank Morgan, Tony Martin, and Meredith Willson — and a special guest, the glorious voice of Miliza Korjus — so don't miss it! See you next Thursday — and in the meantime, go to the movies, and take the family with you. The new Norma Shearer-Clark Gable picture "Idiot's Delight" is opening this week all over the country. Don't miss it! Goodnight!

(MUSIC UP)

HULL: (CREDITS) This is Warren Hull saying goodnight and good luck from the makers of Maxwell House — the coffee that's always good to the last drop.

This is the National Broadcasting Company.

MAXWELL HOUSE
Presents
"GOOD NEWS OF 1940"
February 1, 1940

1. "THERE'S GONNA BE A WEDDING" —ORCHESTRA & CHORUS
2. ARNOLD - WILLSON - COLBERT

    "FAREWELL TO ARMS" —CONNIE BOSWELL
3. COMMERCIAL
4. BABY SNOOKS —FANNY BRICE AND HANLEY STAFFORD
5. "SMOKE GETS IN YOUR EYES" —ORCHESTRA & CHORUS
6. GARGAN-RUBIN SPOT
7. STATION BREAK
8. "AT THE BALALAIKA" —ORCHESTRA & CHORUS
9. "HAPPY YEAR" —COLBERT-ARNOLD-MARSHAL
10. "DARN THAT DREAM" —CONNIE BOSWELL
11. SNOOKS — COMMERCIAL —FANNY BRICE AND HANLEY STAFFORD
12. "THOUGHTS WHILE STROLLING" —ORCHESTRA & CHORUS and SIGN-OFF

HULL: Maxwell House Coffee presents—Good News of 1940!

          (MUSIC IN AND FADE)

ARNOLD: This is Edward Arnold, ladies and gentlemen, and I am happy to welcome you on behalf of the makers of Maxwell House Coffee to another Good News program starring Fanny Brice, Hanley Stafford, Connie Boswell, Benny Rubin, and Meredith Willson and his orchestra. Tonight's program as we promised you last week, is an especially great occasion because we welcome as guests not only Alan Marshall and our good friend, Billy Gargan, but also one of the screen's most talented stars, who is a most captivating lady as well... Miss Claudette Colbert.

MEREDITH:: Gee, Ed, is she really here?

ARNOLD: Yes, Meredith, she's really here. Do you think your heart can stand it?

MEREDITH: I don't know, Ed — but if she's gonna stop, she's gonna stop, that's all. Boy oh boy!

ARNOLD: You're one of Miss Colbert's more devoted fans, I take it.

MEREDITH: Fan ain't the word to describe what I feel toward that sublime creature, Ed.

ARNOLD: No?

MEREDITH: No sir! Would you say Romeo was a fan of Juliet's?

ARNOLD: Well, let's not get into Shakespeare. I'll let you meet Miss Colbert in a minute, but right now suppose you try to get the program started with some music.

MEREDITH:: Okay.

ARNOLD: What are you going to play?

MEREDITH:: I don't know! Whatever the boys have got ready! (MUMBLES INTO IT)

"THERE'S GONNA BE A WEDDIN'"
—ORCHESTRA AND CHORUS

(APPLAUSE)

ARNOLD: That was "There's Gonna Be a Weddin'," played by Meredith Willson and his orchestra — with a tap dance

	routine by Benny Rubin, sitting down. Very good, Meredith, considering your condition.
MEREDITH::	Cut it out, Ed. When are you gonna let me meet the — you know — (SIMPERS) Miss — (SIMPERS)
ARNOLD:	Oh, try to pull yourself together! (MISS COLBERT ENTERS BEHIND MEREDITH)
MEREDITH:	Okay. Is my tie straight?
ARNOLD:	You look all right. Just relax. Now—Miss Colbert, this is Meredith Willson.
MEREDITH:	(LIKE HE'S BEEN SHOT) Where the — Holy Smoke, you might give a guy some warning!
COLBERT:	Is it as bad as all that, Mr. Willson?
MEREDITH:	No, it's wonderful! I beg your pardon — er — I mean I'm pleased to meet you!
ARNOLD:	Meredith, try to act like you've been around!
MEREDITH:	Well I haven't! Gee, Miss Colbert, I can't tell you what this means to me — I mean having an intimate conversation with you, like this.
COLBERT:	Yes, it's marvelous, isn't it?
MEREDITH:	Sure is! Er — what's your favorite hobby, Miss Colbert? (LAUGHS)
COLBERT:	Oh, you tell me yours, first!
MEREDITH:	Promise not to laugh?
COLBERT:	I'll try.
MEREDITH:	Huh?
COLBERT:	I won't laugh. What is *your* favorite hobby? (LAUGHS LIKE HIM)
MEREDITH:	Stamps and coins.
COLBERT:	Oh — numismatics.

MEREDITH: No — I collect nickels.

COLBERT: That's sensible.

MEREDITH: Sure. Say — just so our friendship will ripen faster — Er — would you mind telling me the story of your life?

COLBERT: Tell me yours, first.

MEREDITH: You sure you wanna hear it? I was born in Mason City, Iowa, on March 13, 1908, my dad was a prosperous —

ARNOLD: Meredith!

MEREDITH: What's the matter?

ARNOLD: I know Claudette Colbert hasn't got the heart to stop you, but I have. If you can get her to listen to the story of your life some other time —

MEREDITH: Oh yeah?

COLBERT: I'd love to hear it some other time, Mr. Willson. I think Mr. Arnold wants to get on with the program.

MEREDITH: Oh.

ARNOLD: That's it, exactly, Claudette. Connie Boswell's going to sing for us now — and Connie, I want to congratulate you on winning the annual Radio Daily Poll as America's Number One singer.

CONNIE: Thanks, Eddie.

ARNOLD: Tonight, Connie sings "Farewell to Arms."

"FAREWELL TO ARMS" —CONNIE BOSWELL

(APPLAUSE)

ARNOLD: And now, ladies and gentlemen, here is Fanny Brice as Baby Snooks!

(MUSIC ... APPLAUSE)

ARNOLD:	Well, it looks as though Daddy, played by Hanley Stafford, may get rich. He has discovered a notice in the newspaper calling for the missing heirs of a rich man by the name of Higgins, and Daddy thinks he may be related. So right now we find him hard at work trying to trace his family line. Listen …
FATHER:	(TO HIMSELF) Hmmm … Had no idea my family went that far back … Now, if I can only prove a claim to the old man's fortune … Hmm …
BRICE:	Hello, daddy.
FATHER:	Snooks, you should be in bed.
BRICE:	I ain't sleepy.
FATHER:	Listen, Snooks — I have work to do and I don't want to be disturbed.
BRICE:	What are you doing, Daddy?
FATHER:	I'm looking at some books on genealogy.
BRICE:	Jimmy who?
FATHER:	Not Jimmy — genealogy. "Genea," birth — "ology," discourse. It's taken from the Greek.
BRICE:	Which Greek?
FATHER:	Any Greek!
BRICE:	Parkyakarkus?
FATHER:	What's Parkyakarkus got to do with this?
BRICE:	I dunno.
FATHER:	Genealogy is an account or history of the descent of a person or family from an ancestor! I'm looking up my family tree!
BRICE:	Why?
FATHER:	To find my origin.

BRICE:	Is it an orange tree?
FATHER:	Snooks, maybe I'm just irritable tonight — but you're being very aggravating! Did I say anything about oranges?
BRICE:	Uh-huh.
FATHER:	I did not! I said origin! Origin! Understand?
BRICE:	Understand.
FATHER:	Well, what did I say?
BRICE:	Oranges.
FATHER:	All right — I said oranges — go to bed!
BRICE:	I want an orange.
FATHER:	You can't have any oranges! Will you go to bed and let me finish my work?
BRICE:	What's in the books, daddy?
FATHER:	I just told you. It's the history of all the Higgins' — it tells how our family was founded.
BRICE:	How did it get lost?
FATHER:	I'm talking about the very first Higgins — one of my forefathers.
BRICE:	Did you have four fathers?
FATHER:	Certainly.
BRICE:	Did you have four mothers, too?
FATHER:	(MIMICS HER) No, I didn't have four mothers. I had one mother.
BRICE:	Did they all live together?
FATHER:	Who?
BRICE:	Your one mother and four fathers.

FATHER: My mother had nothing to do with my forefathers!

BRICE: Didn't she like them?

FATHER: Certainly she liked them!

BRICE: Then why didn't she have nothing to do with them?

FATHER: She never met them!

BRICE: Huh?

FATHER: When I say forefathers I don't mean four fathers! Nobody has four fathers but everybody has forefathers and they don't have to be your father at all.

BOTH TOGETHER: Do you feel all right, daddy?

FATHER: I knew that was coming! And don't ask me to explain anything else.

BRICE: Well, why ain't I got four fathers, daddy?

FATHER: Heaven only knows! You could certainly use three more!

BRICE: Why?

FATHER: Because you never listen to anything I tell you.

BRICE: I'll listen, daddy.

FATHER: Well, it's all very simple. The forefathers I'm referring to are my ancestors — they all bore the name of Higgins and they were my progenitors. Savvy?

BRICE: Savvy.

FATHER: Thank Heaven!

BRICE: You had four fathers and they were all janitors.

FATHER: That's fine — you're going to bed goodnight!

BRICE: Goodnight — I'm staying here.

FATHER: Look here, Snooks — this work I'm doing tonight may mean an awful lot to you.

BRICE: Why?

FATHER: Because if I can prove I'm related to a certain man we'll be rich.

BRICE: Which man?

FATHER: An eccentric millionaire who died two weeks ago. His name was Lockstep Higgins.

BRICE: Lockstep Higgins?

FATHER: That's right. It's a very odd first name and that's the one thing that leads me to believe he's a kinsman.

BRICE: Why?

FATHER: Well, it's a characteristic trait of our family to give unique first names. That explains your Uncle Camembert and your little brother Robespierre.

BRICE: What explains me?

FATHER: The less said the better. Anyway, the name seems to be a clue.

BRICE: What's your name, daddy?

FATHER: Oh, you know my name, Snooks.

BRICE: No, I don't.

FATHER: You do, too! What does mother call me?

BRICE: Pinhead.

FATHER: She does not, — and don't remind me of it! My name happens to be the only departure from the list of curious name in our family.

BRICE: Tell me your name, daddy.

FATHER: It's Lancelot Bottlecap Higgins! And you needn't act as if you didn't know!

BRICE:	I knew the Lancelot — but I didn't know the Bottlecap.
FATHER:	Well, I — I don't use my middle name very often.
BRICE:	I like it. Bottlecap, Bottlecap where have you been? I've been to London to—
FATHER:	All right, all right. The main thing is to try and get a portion of the old man's money. It's over five million dollars.
BRICE:	How do you know?
FATHER:	He left a will.
BRICE:	Will Higgins?
FATHER:	No — will. Last will and testament. It's a paper you sign that allows somebody to get all the money you've made.
BRICE:	Did you sign a will with mummy?
FATHER:	What do you mean?
BRICE:	Well, she takes your salary ever —
FATHER:	I know! (Haven't seen the inside of my pay envelope for nine years! Like being married to an installment company).
BRICE:	Huh?
FATHER:	Nothing! Wait till I get my hands on this dough!
BRICE:	Are you gonna get it, daddy?
FATHER:	I don't know. I haven't been able to trace any family connection with this Lockstep Higgins yet.
BRICE:	I'll help you look.
FATHER:	I've been all thru my side of the family. Now I'm going to find out what's on mother's side.
BRICE:	I know what's on mother's side, daddy.
FATHER:	What?

BRICE:	A mustard plaster … I seen her put it there.
FATHER:	I'm not talking about that at all! I've got to look thru her lineage.
BRICE:	The clean ones?
FATHER:	Oh, stop it! Hand me those papers.
BRICE:	What's in this big book, daddy?
FATHER:	That's an old family album. Let me see it — there might be something in it.
BRICE:	(LAUGHS) Look at the funny pictures!
FATHER:	What's funny about them? They're just wearing old-fashioned clothes, that's all. But you can see that every member of my family was an aristocrat.
BRICE:	A rusty cat?
FATHER:	Aristocrat! Plenty of blue blood in my veins!
BRICE:	Is there?
FATHER:	Certainly! I'll let you in on a little secret, Snooks — I come from a family of peers!
BRICE:	I won't tell nobody, daddy.
FATHER:	Oh, I'm proud of it!
BRICE:	Why?
FATHER:	Why? Look at the picture of this fine old gentleman — one of my great-grandfathers. This was taken when he was made a knight.
BRICE:	How did he look in the daytime?
FATHER:	He looked fine! Queen Elizabeth made him knight. She gave him the Order of the Bath.
BRICE:	Did he take it?
FATHER:	Of course — it's a great honor. He was thirty years old

	at the time and he never expected to get the Order of the Bath.
BRICE:	He never got it before?
FATHER:	Of course not.
BRICE:	He must have been awful dirty.
FATHER:	The Order of the Bath is a title! It's like being a prince!
BRICE:	Ohhhh … . Who's this one, daddy?
FATHER:	Oh. We — er — we never speak of him. He was my father's uncle. Let me tear that picture up, Snooks.
BRICE:	Is that the one who was a bearded lady in the circus?
FATHER:	Yes, he ran aw——how did you know?
BRICE:	Mummy shows it to everybody.
FATHER:	Oh, she does, eh! Well, I'll go around showing pictures of her relatives if I can get them out of the Rogues Gallery!
BRICE:	I wanna see 'em, daddy.
FATHER:	Never mind! What's that you've got in your hand?
BRICE:	It's a funny picture with writing on it.
FATHER:	Let me see. (READS) To Cousin Flyleaf — that's my father — from Cousin Lockstep Higgins. Lockstep! That's the guy!
BRICE:	Who?
FATHER:	The millionaire! Snooks! We're rich!
BRICE:	Are we?
FATHER:	I'll inherit a fortune! Where's that lawyer's phone number? Here! Let me get at that phone!
BRICE:	Here, daddy.

FATHER:	(RECEIVER OFF) Hello — hello. Get me State 40101! I knew that Lockstep would be a member of my family! He had brains.
BRICE:	Why?
FATHER:	He must have had brains to make five million dollars. That's the stuff us Higgins are made of! It runs in the family!
BRICE:	Runs in the family?
FATHER:	You bet! We're all alike — every one of us! Hello … This is Lancelot Higgins calling about the — huh? What? He didn't leave a cent! But the will — ohh! He was nuts, eh?
BRICE:	Does it run in the family, daddy?
FATHER:	I see — goodbye (HANGS UP) Well, that's that! The old loon was broke (SADLY) Everything happens to me.
BRICE:	Go to bed, daddy.
FATHER:	Okay. (ALMOST SOBBING) Goodnight, Snooks.
BRICE:	Goodnight … … Poor daddy! (LAUGHS) WAAAAAHHHHH!
	(MUSIC … APPLAUSE)
ARNOLD:	Now — another of Meredith Willson's spectacular production arrangements. This time he's chosen one of Jerome Kern's most magical melodies, and made of it a dazzlingly brilliant musical experience. Meredith presents — "Smoke Gets in Your Eyes."
	"SMOKE GETS IN YOUR EYES" —ORCHESTRA
	(APPLAUSE)
ARNOLD:	Very good, Meredith! Very good indeed! Now, ladies and gentlemen, we're very happy to welcome again a young man who's becoming very popular on this program—Joe Turp, otherwise known as Bill Gargan!

(APPLAUSE)

GARGAN: Thank you, Edward. Good evening, everybody. It's a pleasure to attend such a distinguished gathering of bon vivants.

ARNOLD: That ain't the Gargan I know. Let your hair down, Turp!

GARGAN: Please, Edward! Not tonight!

ARNOLD: Aren't you gonna do a Joe Turp story?

GARGAN: No. I think it would be wise, Edward, for the public to hear me as my natural cultivated self. So I'll ask you to forget all about Brooklyn — at last for the nonce.

ARNOLD: Whatever you say, old fellow. I can understand your feelings.

RUBIN: Pardon me, Buddy—I'm soiching for a party by the name of William Gargan.

GARGAN: William Gargan? I am he.

RUBIN: I am he. Yes sir. Here's a package from the Express Company, sign here. Buck and a half, C.O.D.

GARGAN: Oh, thanks. Wait till I get my wallet.

RUBIN: Say, you ain't *Bill* Gargan, are you pal?

GARGAN: I am he.

RUBIN: Bill Gargan from Brooklyn?

GARGAN: I am he.

ARNOLD: I am — going. (HE GOES)

RUBIN: Hey, Mr. Gargan, I'm from back there too! Atlantic Avenue!

GARGAN: No kiddin', are you from Brooklyn?

RUBIN: I am he! (THEY SHAKE HANDS) I seen you in a lotta pictures, Mr. Gargan—but don't I know your kisser from some place back home?

GARGAN: I don't think so.

RUBIN: Lemme think ... Use you go to the Philharmonic Concerts at the Academy?

GARGAN: Soitenly — I use. Use you?

RUBIN: Use you?

GARGAN: Sure, I use!

RUBIN: Use you go to the concerts in the park, too?

GARGAN: Yah, I use. Use you?

RUBIN: Dat's where I seen ya. Remember that night when Stokowski was knockin' off that Bach fugue in F sharp minor?

GARGAN: I was there! I was there and I didn't miss a note from the foist andante down tru all de codas up to the fortissimo.

RUBIN: Wasn't it de nuts?

GARGAN: But I tell ya what's missin' with Stokowski. It's all right to use your bare hands when you're conductin', but ya gotta remember that baton holds a great significance to a musician, because some of dem guys like to be bulldozed!

RUBIN: You're right ... and while we're takin' a rap at Leo, you know what I miss in him that Toscanini has got? That underground of lascivious harmonization dat's always prevalent when the wind instruments play a la legato.

GARGAN: Buddy, let me shake the hand of a guy with a soul!

RUBIN: Oh, dat's all right. Say ... how do ya like the Apres-Mi-D'un Faun by de Bussy?

GARGAN: Apres-Mi-D'un Faun?

RUBIN: Yah! That's when the sheep take it on the lamb in a park!

GARGAN: (ENTHUSIASTICALLY) Yah! I know. They run all over the joint. Take the foist theme. You know, the one announced by the flute?

RUBIN: It's hittin' me.

GARGAN: When the strings rise up in their celestial splendor culminatin' in that dominant ninth chord!

RUBIN: You mean the inverted dominant ninth chord?

GARGAN: Yah- how did I ever leave dat out?

RUBIN: I tell ya, when I hear dat — I could go without eatin'!

GARGAN: You know what I miss out here something terrible?

RUBIN: Chamber music —

GARGAN: No, Opera. There ain't nothing out here like the Met. I got so starved for beauty I even listen to the radio.

RUBIIN: Ya kiddin'!

GARGAN: No! I tell ya who I heard de other day … Round-Tone-Larry.

RUBIN: Who?

GARGAN: Larry Tibbet!

RUBIN: That's my idea of a baritone.

GARGAN: It gives me pleasure to hear you say that. I hoid him blast out Figgarro.

RUBIN: Why, I hold it a thousand times!

GARGAN: Yah? But not with Tibbet's fullness — not with the color — not with the shading — the enunciation — why he practically narrates the story for you.

RUBIN: That's right. I'm nuts about him and John Chuck Thomas — especially when Chuck at the finish of a concert says "Goodnight, mother." I tell ya — something — it tears the cockles of my heart.

GARGAN: (REVERENTLY) Yah, it's inspirin'!

RUBIN: Well I gotta get back to me truck. Ya didn't pay me for the C.O.D.

GARGAN: Here y'are. Say — don't tell nobody what's in it.

RUBIN: How would I know? I only deliver 'em, I don't wrap 'em.

GARGAN: Okay. Forget it.

RUBIN: Soitenly. What is it?

GARGAN: I ain't sayin'!

RUBIN: What are you ashamed of?

GARGAN: I ain't ashamed of nothin'. But I ain't just sayin'. That's all.

RUBIN: Is it hot?

GARGAN: Wait a minute, Buddy — I never stole nothing in my life. And I would tell ya what it is if I was sure ya wouldn't say nothin' to nobody.

RUBIN: I won't say a word. What is it?

GARGAN: Well, it's embarrassing.

RUBIN: Okay, then. Don't tell me.

GARGAN: I'll tell ya but if ya ever say anything to anyone …

RUBIN: Honor bright! I won't open my kisser.

GARGAN: (HESITATINGLY) Well … it's … … .a flute.

RUBIN: (SURPRISED) A flute?

GARGAN: Yah — a silver flute.

RUBIN: Can ya play it?

GARGAN: Soitenly!

RUBIN: That's wonderful. Give me a load!

"GOOD NEWS OF 1940" — February 1, 1940

GARGAN: Yah — wait a minute — give me a chance to warm up my lip. I ain't practiced for a long time. (PLAYS A COUPLE OF STACCATO NOTES) Here's a cadenza for ya. (HE PLAYS A CADENZA.)

RUBIN: What a glissando! That's the hottest lip I ever hoid!

GARGAN: Thanks, Buddy. I'm glad ya appreciate it.

RUBIN: Now that ya opened up — I've got a little confessin' to do myself.

GARGAN: Yah? What is it?

RUBIN: Well — I do some singin'. (IN A DIFFERENT PITCH) Well, I do some singin'. (IN ANOTHER DIFFERENT PITCH) Well, I do some singin'. (IN STILL ANOTHER PITCH) Well, I do some singin'. (IN STILL ANOTHER PITCH) Well, I do some singin'.

GARGAN: Got a good range, ain't you?

RUBIN: Yeah. I'm a baritone. (SINGS "SHORTENIN BREAD")

GARGAN: Say, you got real class! Maybe we can rip off a dust.

RUBIN: Yah. By the way, do you know a very popular song that's out just now — "Lo, Hear the Gentle Lark"?

GARGAN: Yah. I know that. How's dat key? (HE PLAYS FOUR BARS OF "LO, HEAR THE GENTLE LARK")

RUBIN: That's ok with me. Go ahead — get started!

RUBIN: (SINGS "LO, HEAR THE GENTLE LARK" WITH FLUTE ECHOS AFTER EACH PHRASE, FINISHING WITH A TYPICAL POP FINISH OF "GOOD EVENING, FRIENDS.")

GARGAN : Great, Buddy. Glad to have met ya!

RUBIN: Okay. I'll see ya at the ballet.

(MUSIC UP)

(APPLAUSE)

ARNOLD:	This is Edward Arnold again, and we continue our Good News with Claudette Colbert, Fanny Brice, Hanley Stafford, Connie Boswell and Meredith Willson. Meredith opens our second act with a song from the new Nelson Eddy-Ilona Massey picture, MGM's "Balalaika." It's called simply "At the Balalaika."
	"AT THE BALALAIKA" —ORCHESTRA
	(APPLAUSE)
ARNOLD:	It is now my extreme pleasure to present our lovely guest, Claudette Colbert, in a dramatic sketch entitled "Happy Year" by Arch Oboler. With Miss Colbert you will hear Alan Marshal as Ed Blake, and I will do my best to portray the part of the Prosecuting Attorney. Meredith — will you ring up the curtain.
	THEATER OF THE AIR
GARGAN:	This is Bill Gargan from Brooklyn, butting in, ladies and gentlemen — and I just want to say I think Claudette Colbert and Eddie Arnold gave two very beautiful performances in Mr. Oboler's dramatic sketch. Now — another gifted performer — my pal Connie Boswell. Connie, it's a pity you weren't born in Brooklyn.
CONNIE:	You shoulda come from New Orleans, Bill!
GARGAN:	Well, we're both here now, anyway! Ladies and gentlemen, Connie Boswell sings "Darn That Dream."
	"DARN THAT DREAM" —ORCHESTRA & BOSWELL
	(APPLAUSE)
	CONCERT HALL THEME
ARNOLD:	The melody you are now hearing, which is the theme of our Concert Hall, was written by Meredith Willson in honor of a great and beloved man. Since this melody

was written, that man has passed on. It is timely, this month that we spend a moment paying tribute to him.. In the Concert Hall, Meredith Willson presents "Thoughts While Strolling" from his own suite dedicated to O. O. MacIntyre.

"THOUGHTS WHILE STROLLING" — ORCHESTRA

(APPLAUSE)

ARNOLD: Next week, ladies and gentlemen, another treat. We will have with us a man all Hollywood loves, a man whose marvelous performances on the screen have endeared him to all America. That splendid gentlemen, Ronald Colman.

(APPLAUSE)

Ronald will appear in a special preview of Paramount's new picture "The Light That Failed" and with him as additional guests we will have Ida Lupino and Muriel Angelus. Of course, all our regular cast will be back again — irrepressible Fanny Brice as Baby Snooks with Hanley Stafford as Daddy — America's favorite singer of popular songs, Connie Boswell and Meredith Willson and his orchestra. It's a show I don't want to miss, so I'll be here too ... I hope you'll make it a date with us. Until next Thursday then, this is Edward saying — Goodnight.

("ALWAYS AND ALWAYS" FADES)

MAXWELL HOUSE
Presents
"GOOD NEWS OF 1940"
February 8, 1940

1. "LET'S ALL SING TOGETHER" —ORCHESTRA & CHORUS
2. WILLSON - ARNOLD - COLMAN
   "STORMY WEATHER" —CONNIE BOSWELL
3. COMMERCIAL
4. BABY SNOOKS —FANNY BRICE AND HANLEY STAFFORD
5. "YOURS IS MY HEART ALONE" —FRANK PARKER
6. RUBIN-GARGAN SPOT
7. STATION BREAK
8. "THE LIGHT THAT FAILED" —RONALD COLMAN - IDA LUPINO - MURIEL ANGELUS
9. COMMERCIAL —SNOOKS
10. CONCERT HALL and SIGN OFF

HULL: Maxwell House Coffee presents ... Good News of 1940!

(MUSIC IN AND FADE)

ARNOLD: This is Edward Arnold, ladies and gentlemen, and on behalf of the makers of Maxwell House Coffee I welcome you to another hour of Good News, starring Fanny Brice, William Gargan, Hanley Stafford, Benny Rubin, Connie Boswell, and Meredith Willson and his Orchestra.

(MUSIC OUT)

	We have with us also this evening a distinguished group of guests — stars of the William A. Wellman Paramount production "The Light That Failed," Mr. Ronald Colman, Miss Ida Lupino, and Miss Muriel Angelus. And as an added attraction we are glad to welcome a radio singer I know you all like — Frank Parker. For his opening number Meredith has something special, I daresay.
MEREDITH:	Sure have. It's called "The Spirit of Swing." Ready, boys?

ORCHESTRA NUMBER (TWO BARS)

(APPLAUSE)

ARNOLD:	That was very good, Meredith.
COLMAN:	Yes, very good indeed — but wasn't it a little on the short side?
ARNOLD:	Ronald Colman!

(APPLAUSE)

MEREDITH:	Mr. Colman? Willson's the name. Two ells.
COLMAN:	How do you do?
MEREDITH:	I notice you noticed my opening number was a little short. The explanation for that is, I'd like to have a word with you in regards to a certain matter.
COLMAN:	All right old boy. Go ahead.
MEREDITH:	Well I — well I — I want to act, in the worst way.
COLMAN:	I beg your pardon?
MEREDITH:	Romantic, swashbuckling types. You know, like Dodsworth. Could you give me an audition?
COLMAN:	Well let me see. An audition. I have it!
MEREDITH:	What?

COLMAN:	It happens I seldom go anywhere without a piece of verse.
MEREDITH:	You mean poetry?
COLMAN:	Yes! Are you familiar with Omar Khayam?
MEREDITH:	What was the name?
COLMAN:	Omar Khayam.
MEREDITH:	Fella that made the tents?
COLMAN:	No, no tents. Omar Khayam was a poet, and he wrote The Rubaiyat.
MEREDITH:	Okay, okay.
COLMAN:	I have a stanza from the Rubaiyat in my pocket. I got it off a calendar.
MEREDITH:	A calendar, it must be good.
COLMAN:	Just what I thought. Now you read it to me. Here.
MEREDITH:	Thanks. (CLEARS THROAT) Do you want it with an English accent, or regular?
COLMAN:	Oh — just regular?
MEREDITH:	Okay. I sure admire that accent of yours, Mr. Colman.
COLMAN:	Thank you.
MEREDITH:	It's a darb!
COLMAN:	Thank you. Now let me hear you read.
MEREDITH:	Okay. (READS) "Ah, moon of my delight, who know'st no wane, "The moon of heav'n is rising once agen."
COLMAN:	Quite a rhyme, isn't it?
MEREDITH:	I ain't finished.
COLMAN:	No no, I mean it will rhyme if you pronounce it "again."

MEREDITH: Oh. Pardon me. (READS FASTER THIS TIME)
"Ah moon of my delight who know'st no wane
"The moon of heav'n is rising once again."
It worked!

COLMAN: Bravo! Go on!

MEREDITH: (READS) "How oft hereafter rising shall she look
"Through this same garden after me in vain,
"Compliments of the Beverly Hills Ice Company."

COLMAN: Magnificent! I'll see what I can do for you — but not now!

(APPLAUSE)

ARNOLD: Ladies and gentlemen, by public demand — once again Miss Connie Boswell brings us her superb arrangement of Harold Arlen's great song, "Stormy Weather."

"STORMY WEATHER" —BOSWELL AND ORCHESTRA

(APPLAUSE)

FIRST HALF OF SHOW

ARNOLD: Before introducing Warren Hull ... I'd like you to hear a letter we very much appreciate. It's from a lady who said a great deal in two short sentences. She is Mrs. Erma K. Schade of Rockford, Illinois. Said Mrs. Schade:

WOMAN: My family demands perfect coffee. Elimination of the less than perfect coffees left only Maxwell House — rich, fragrant ... perfect!

ARNOLD: And now, here's Warren Hull to tell us just why Maxwell House is so good, so downright satisfying ...

HULL: Well, friends, we've found a way to blend Maxwell House to a new perfection of flavor ... a full-bodied mellow flavor that comes form very special coffees ... highland-grown coffees from remote and fertile plantations of Central and South America. And then ...

	to bring out the true, natural goodness of this matchless new blend, we've developed a remarkable process called Radiant Roast … a process which uses uniform, penetrating heat to roast each coffee-bean evenly all the way thru. This way, there's no chance of weak coffee from under- roasting … or bitter coffee from parched coffee beans. All the rare and mellow flavor of this superb new blend is brought to its peak in every cup you serve. That's why … today … more people are enjoying Maxwell House Coffee than ever before in its history … why more stores sell Maxwell House than any other coffee in America!
HULL:	So, if you haven't tried Maxwell House lately, ask for a pound tomorrow … won't you? Compare it with what you now think is "good" coffee. We think you, too, will say … Here's perfect coffee … coffee that's now, more than ever … Good to the Last Drop!
	(MUSIC BRIDGE)
ARNOLD:	And now, ladies and gentlemen, here is Fanny Brice as Baby Snooks!
	(MUSIC … APPLAUSE)
ARNOLD:	Daddy, played by Hanley Stafford, has been a man of mystery for the past few nights. As soon as he finishes dinner he locks himself in his makeshift laboratory and allows nobody to enter. As the scene opens we find him entering his little room in the basement. Listen … …
SOUND:	(DOOR CLOSES … KEY IN LOCK)
FATHER:	That's that! Guess that'll keep those busy-bodies out!
BRICE:	Hello, daddy.
FATHER:	Snooks! How did you get here? I thought you were still in the dining room.
BRICE:	Did you?
FATHER:	Yes! I want to know how you got in here!

BRICE: I made myself into a spit-ball and I rolled thru the keyhole.

FATHER: Oh, you did, eh? Well — roll right out again.

BRICE: I wanna stay here, daddy.

FATHER: All right. But if I let you stay here you must promise not to bother me even for a second. Promise?

BRICE: Promise.

FATHER: And no matter what you see in this room tonight I want you to be as silent as a tomb.

BRICE: Silent.

FATHER: Snooks — you see that big thing in the corner? Covered with a sheet.

BRICE: Uh-huh. What is it?

FATHER: I'm building a robot.

BRICE: Huh?

FATHER: I'm building a robot.

BRICE: Who's gonna row it, daddy?

FATHER: Not a rowboat — a robot! It's a mechanical man that talks like a human being — moves like a human — but looks like a jumbled mess and has no brains. Now do you know what it is?

BRICE: Uncle Louie.

FATHER: No! It's an automaton. It responds only to the commands of the operator. I've been working on it secretly for the past four months.

BRICE: Why?

FATHER: Because it's a dream of mine — and if it comes true we'll be rich! I'll never have to work again and brother, will I tell everybody where to go!

BRICE:	Where?
FATHER:	It doesn't matter.
BRICE:	(WITH MEANING) I know where.
FATHER:	Never mind! I'm just hoping this robot will work properly — but I don't want to count my chickens before they're hatched.
BRICE:	Can he lay eggs, too?
FATHER:	No, he can't lay eggs!
BRICE:	I wanna see him.
FATHER:	You will in just a minute, Snooks, I want to check my plans and see if I've overlooked anything.
BRICE:	Can I lift up the sheet and have a peek?
FATHER:	No.
BRICE:	Just a teeny weeny little peek?
FATHER::	I don't want you to see it until I unveil it.
BRICE:	Can I feel it?
FATHER:	No — you can't feel it!
BRICE:	Well — can I smell it?
FATHER:	No! No peeking, no feeling and no smelling!
BRICE:	Any sniffing?
FATHER:	Stay away from that robot! I've worked on it too long to have you ruin it.
BRICE:	How did you make it, daddy?
FATHER:	Well, to begin with I made a very careful study of the human anatomy.
BRICE:	What's that?
FATHER:	Have you ever seen a skeleton?

BRICE: Uh-huh. I seen one in the doctor's office.

FATHER: Fine. Then you know what a skeleton is.

BRICE: It's a man with his outside off and his inside sticking out.

FATHER: That's close enough. Well, in order to understand the movements of the extremities I had to read an entire chapter on syndesmology.

BRICE: Syndesmology?

FATHER: Yes, joints. I spent two nights going thru the joints.

BRICE: Did you take mummy?

FATHER: Mummy didn't know anything about it!

BRICE: Is that why she hollered?

FATHER: (YELLS) Nobody hollered! Syndesmology is the scientific term for the study of development of the joints. And ligaments.

BRICE: Oh.

FATHER: I had to learn about the joints to make the robot move properly. Then I examined the construction of the brain and cranium.

BRICE: Why?

FATHER: Because the brain controls all the sections. It's made up of sections called lobes. There's the frontal, temporal, parietal and occipital. That means the front, side, top and back. Think you can remember that?

BRICE: Uh-huh.

FATHER: Well, what are they?

BRICE: The frontal, side-al, topple and backle.

FATHER: That's better than I expected. Anyway — to make the robot look very natural I put in veins and arteries made of rubber — to show the circulation of the blood.

BRICE:	What's that?
FATHER:	Well, you know how the bloodstream keeps moving in the body. For instance, when I stand on my head —
BRICE:	Stand on your head, daddy.
FATHER:	Not now. When I stand on my head — all the blood rushes there and fills it. But when I stand up straight the blood doesn't rush to my feet. You know why?
BRICE:	'Cause your feet ain't empty.
FATHER:	That's not the reason at all! It's because there is less pressure when the heart is pumping in its normal direction. I think.
BRICE:	I wanna see the rowboat!
FATHER:	Robot!
BRICE:	I wanna see him!
FATHER:	Just a few seconds now. I want to explain him first so you won't be completely mystified. Naturally, he's run by electricity — but I've put glass inspection windows all over his body so you can see how he works. He has one of those little panes on his head — one on his feet and so forth.
BRICE:	Has he got a pane in his stomach?
FATHER:	Yes, Snooks, I'm going to unveil him now. Step over here.
BRICE:	Awight, daddy.
FATHER:	Here we go — let me get this sheet off, and you'll really be proud of your old dad. There! There's my robot! (PAUSE)
BRICE:	Do you feel all right, daddy?
FATHER:	I feel fine! What's the matter with him?
BRICE:	I'm gonna tell mummy you took her wash-boiler.

FATHER:	You stay here! It's the only material I had to work with.
BRICE:	Why is he holding that coffee pot?
FATHER:	That's the whole idea! That's what's going to make me rich!
BRICE:	How?
FATHER:	Well, I'm going to take him to the Maxwell House coffee people and they can use him for advertising. See — he's got the coffee-pot in one hand and a cup and saucer in the other.
BRICE:	Uh-huh.
FATHER:	Now — when I press the button he pours a cup of coffee and says "Will you have a cup of Maxwell House coffee — it's good to the last drop."
BRICE:	Let me hear him say it.
FATHER:	Well, I haven't tested it yet — but I'm sure it will work. You'd never believe how I made the voice.
BRICE:	I'll believe it, daddy.
FATHER:	I took the horn off of our car and attached it to him. When I press the button, the horn blows a steady note and the lips move to form the words.
BRICE:	Will you have a cup of Maxwell House Coffee it's good to the last drop?
FATHER:	Exactly! Watch! I'll press the button.
SOUND:	(JUST AN AUTO HORN)
BRICE:	Are you sure you feel all right, daddy?
FATHER:	I don't understand it! The lips moved and everything.
BRICE:	Can he move as good as he talks, daddy?
FATHER:	Oh, he'll move all right! I'm certain of that! Watch him pour the coffee.

BRICE: I'm watching.

FATHER: Here's the button. There!

SOUND: (CRASH AS THE THING FALLS APART)

BRICE: Good to the last drop!

FATHER: Well! There goes five months labor — and a dollar eight in materials ... (SADLY) I guess you think I'm altogether cracked, don't you, Snooks?

BRICE: No, daddy.

FATHER: Thank Heaven.

BRICE: Not altogether.

FATHER: Oh. Listen — I don't care so much about the failure of this thing — but I don't want mother to find out. If you promise not to tell her — I'll give you this dime.

BRICE: I don't want the dime, daddy.

FATHER: Snooks! What's come over you? You don't want this bright, new shiny dime?

BRICE: No. But I'll keep my trap shut for a greasy old dollar!

FATHER: Oh, you will, eh! Well, you can blab all you like — and here's something to start you off! (SLAP)

BRICE: WAAAAAAAAHHHHHHHH!

(MUSIC ... APPLAUSE)

ARNOLD: In the Concert Hall tonight, it is a great pleasure to present a special Valentine gift to our Maxwell House friends. We are happy to bring you Frank Parker, whom I personally nominate as one of the great artists of our times, singing Frank Lehar's loveliest song, "Yours Is My Heart Alone" — We pay tribute to a fine singer, and a fine song — All right, Meredith —

"YOURS IS MY HEART ALONE" —PARKER, ORCHESTRA & CHORUS

ARNOLD:	Very good, Mr. Parker! Now, ladies and gentlemen, that charming young gentleman is now a regular member of our Good News family — Mr. Bill Gargan!
	(APPLAUSE)
GARGAN:	Thank you. Good evening, ladies and gentlemen.
ARNOLD:	Bill, are we to look forward to another Joe Turp sketch this evening?
GARGAN:	Please, Edward! I begged you last week to forget about my Brooklyn accent. Very few people know this, but in truth, it's all assumed.
ARNOLD:	You mean the way you're talking now is really natural.
GARGAN:	Soitenly. I mean of course. (That's a tough word to shake). Besides, I think it's very important for the radio audience to think of me as a cultivated fellow — the Harvard type. Twig?
ARNOLD:	Well, you can put on a fancy accent if you like. I don't care if you —
RUBIN:	(WORRIED) Oh, there y'are Mr. Gargan! I been looking all over for you! Hello, Mr. Arnold!
ARNOLD:	Hello. More packages from the express company?
RUBIN:	No, I took the afternoon off. I gotta talk to Mr. Gargan about a very intimate matter.
ARNOLD:	Well I'll leave you two Brooklyn boys together. Don't forget your Harvard accent, Bill! (LAUGHS AND WALKS OUT)
GARGAN:	Never fear, old fellow! What is it, Benny?
RUBIN:	Never thought I'd get in to see you, Mr. Gargan! Couldn't get by that doorman out there!
GARGAN:	You had difficulties with the commissionaire?
RUBIN:	Huh?

GARGAN:	The Cerberus at the entrance refused you admittance?
RUBIN:	Gimme a break, Bill! I ain't getting a word of this!
GARGAN:	Oh. You mean that crumb on the gate stiffed you?
RUBIN:	Yeah! He wouldn't lemme tru!
GARGAN:	I'll give him his lumps later. What's eatin' you, Rubin?
RUBIN:	Mr. Gargan, today I come as a harbinger of mercy!
GARGAN:	A harbinger of mercy! In Brooklyn that only means a touch! Goodbye.
RUBIN:	It ain't for me, Mr. Gargan!
GARGAN:	No?
RUBIN:	No. Use you go to P.S. 77 in Foist Street?
GARGAN:	Yes, I use. Use you?
RUBIN:	Soitenly I use. Use you know a guy in school name Al Kochendoerfer.
GARGAN:	Corky? Soitenly I use. Use you?
RUBIN:	Use I? That's what I'm here for!
GARGAN:	Nice kid. What's Corky doin' now?
RUBIN:	Bill — Corky's in a jam! I gotta letter from him this morning. His sister wrote it.
GARGAN:	That's Corky.
RUBIN::	Yeah. Sweet kid, though. Can you imagine Corky in the clink?
GARGAN:	No!
RUBIN:	Yeah! Sweet kid.
GARGAN:	What was the rap?
RUBIN:	Burglary, second degree.

GARGAN: Did he cop a plea?

RUBIN: How could he? The kid's a three-time loser.

GARGAN: Sweet kid.

RUBIN: Yeah. He give in to his old weakness again a couple of weeks ago, and the cops nabbed him! He is now in the Tombs, and he needs eighteen dollars for bail.

GARGAN: Bad, ain't it? What's this about his old weakness, Benny?

RUBIN: You remember! When you was in 6-B, use you hafta go to the Metropolitan Art Museum every Wednesday afternoon?

GARGAN: Sure I use! With Miss Peckinpangle!

RUBIN: Check! Well you know the first time all the kids went to the Metropolitan, Al Kochendoerfer swiped $40 worth of minnatures!

GARGAN: Minnatures?

RUBIN: Them little pictures.

GARGAN: Oh soitenly! Like the Gettysburg address on the head of a pin!

RUBIN: That's it. The principal squared the rap for him! But two years after he got outta school, he histed an art gallery on Fifty Seventh Street, and he —

GARGAN: I recall. He done a two-year stretch.

RUBIN: Check. But it didn't do him no good. He ain't two days down from Ossining when he's walking along Madison Avenue and he sees a Rembrandt in Sloane's window.

GARGAN: I recall. A brick, and he's back in the clink.

RUBIN: Check.

RUBIN: He got out four weeks ago, and he's going in Namm's basement to buy a shirt — and just his luck, they're having a sculpture exhibition.

GARGAN:	Sculpture! Them things weigh a ton! Don't tell me he tried to cop a statue!
RUBIN:	In broad daylight. They caught him going through the basement door with Rodin's Thinker under his coat.
GARGAN:	What an art lover! But it shows you about human nature, don't it? Them Wednesday afternoons at the Metropolitan Museum made Corky a thief.
RUBIN:	Yeah. Now take me for example. Then Wednesday afternoons made me a connoisseur.
GARGAN:	Me too! I learned to appreciate beauty in the abstract.
RUBIN:	Well, abstract is okay if you're cubistically inclined — but me, I'm nuts about nudes.
GARGAN:	I don't mind a nice nude, myself. But my first love is composition and color.
RUBIN:	Very necessary. Are you familiar with that great work of Gainsborough's, Little Boy Blue?
GARGAN:	Pardon me. Gainsborough's Blue Boy. I am very familiar with such work.
RUBIN:	I stand corrected. Well if you'll look closely at the picture, you'll see that the blue in the pants —
GARGAN:	Britches.
RUBIN:	Yeah. Well the color on the right thigh, above the knee, is a robin's egg blue — and on the left leg, in about the same position diametrically, the color takes on an azure tinge.
GARGAN:	You mean the pants don't match?
RUBIN:	Precisely.
GARGAN:	Gainsborough was a phony!
RUBIN:	You're right, Bill. But I'll tell you who's a worse one.
GARGAN:	Who's that?

RUBIN:	Whistler. You know the picture Whistler's Mother.
GARGAN:	Know it like a brother.
RUBIN:	Am I right?
GARGAN:	Benny, I don't like to argue with a connoisseur — but in brief, no. Whistler's Mother is a masterpiece.
RUBIN:	I think you're full of wet hay — but I'm open-minded. Enlighten me.
GARGAN:	Gladly. Close your eyes. Behold the painting of Whistler's Mother. Visualize it.
RUBIN:	I can see it like Whistler is there whistling, right beside her.
GARGAN:	Benny, you're a good visualizer. Now, that ain't just the picture of an old lady. There's a lot behind it. There's a mood, that he captured, but you didn't.
RUBIN:	Uh-uh.
GARGAN:	Notice in your mind's eye the expression. She is thinking of her boy. (SWEETLY) Is he cominghome tonight? If so, what time? Is he in bad company? Trying to get the one-ball in the side pocket? Or is he maybe the lookout for a couple of guys jimmying a store? Where is my boy? What can he be doing? — Where is that bum?
RUBIN:	Can I open my eyes now?
GARGAN:	Yeah. Now don't you get a better perspective on "Whistler's Mother"?
RUBIN:	Yes, I do. It grips me right in the heart. (HALF CRYING) My mudder goes through the same thing every night.
GARGAN:	So you see my boy, every painter catches a different mood. The only ones I can't swally are the surrealists.
RUBIN:	That's where our opinions converge in opposite directions. I'm for the surrealists, body and soul.

GARGAN: Enlighten me.

RUBIN: Listen, I seen a surrealistic mural that was dynamite. Close your eyes.

GARGAN: What for?

RUBIN: I want you to visualize.

GARGAN: All right. I'm in repose.

RUBIN: Picture! There's a mural. There's a girl's face with two creampuffs coming out of her eyes, her mouth is open, out of which come two whales, one smaller than the other. In her hands she's holding a circular saw, with a jack of spades on every point. On her head is a typewriter and on every key is a different vegetable, finishing with a cheese soufflé. Now, what do you think the title is?

GARGAN: What?

RUBIN: Democracy. Do you feel it?

GARGAN: It's surging through me. I'd like to get a gander at that mural. When can we go?

RUBIN: You name the day. Oh say — before I forget — can you help me out for Al Kochendoerfer?

GARGAN: I forgot all about him! How much does he need?

RUBIN: Eighteen bucks'll spring him.

GARGAN: Put me down for the whole works. I'll give you a check right now.

RUBIN: That's swell!

GARGAN: Think nothing of it! Us art-lovers has got to stick together!

(MUSIC ... APPLAUSE)

ARNOLD: Ah ... there's that wonderful fragrance of freshly-brewed Maxwell House Coffee in the air ... and it

	tells me … (LOUD CRASH OF FALLING CHINA FOLLOWED BY HOWL FROM SNOOKS) Snooks! Warren! What's happening?
HULL:	Well, Eddie, I told Snooks she could help me serve the coffee tonight … and …
SNOOKS:	(TEARFULLY) I couldn't help it, Mr. Hull … honest I couldn't. (PAUSE) I tripped! (MORE HOWLING)
HULL:	Oh cheer up, Snooks … it might have been worse. You broke only the cups and saucers. I still have the coffee.
ARNOLD:	Thank goodness for that!
HULL:	And now friends … while Daddy goes backstage for more cups … pull up your chairs. Get ready to enjoy with us a steaming, fragrant cup of Maxwell House Coffee. And with it … the music of Meredith Willson … music as rich and mellow as Maxwell House itself. Meredith …
	(MUSIC FULL AND FADE)
HULL:	We pause briefly for Station Identification.
	(MUSIC FULL AND FADE)
ARNOLD:	This is Edward Arnold and we continue our Good News Maxwell House Show with a special preview of William A. Wellman's Paramount Production of the Rudyard Kipling classic, "The Light That Failed," which stars Ronald Colman, with Walter Huston, Ida Lupino, Muriel Angelus and Dudley Diggs." For our radio premiere we are happy to bring to the air Mr. Colman, Ida Lupino and Muriel Angelus, in the characters they played in the picture … "The Light That Failed."

THEATRE OF THE AIR

ARNOLD:	The story of "The Light That Failed" concerns the undying friendship of two men, Dick Holdar, played by Ronald Colman, and Torpenhow, a war correspondent.

And the love of a man for a woman. You will hear Ida Lupino in the role of Bessie, and Muriel Angelus as Maisie, the lifetime sweetheart. But let us listen to the man who knows the story better than any other ...

THE LIGHT THAT FAILED

ARNOLD: Ronald Colman, Ida Lupino, and Muriel Angelus ... Thank you and congratulations on a fine performance of Paramount's picture "The Light That Failed." I know that after hearing our radio preview of the show tonight all of you will want to see the whole picture, coming to your theatre soon. The part of Torpenhow, originally played by Walter Huston, was portrayed tonight by Frank Nelson. Maisie as a little girl was played by Sarita Wooten and the boy Dick, by Billy Cook. The radio version was prepared by Robert Riley Crutcher, and from the screen by Robert Carsan.

(INTO COMMERCIAL)

ARNOLD: And now, here's Warren Hull, who warns me that, to get all the coffee flavor I pay for, I should beware of coffee which has stood on my grocer's shelves for a day or more, imperfectly protected from air!

HULL: That's right, Eddie.

ARNOLD: And why?

HULL: Because of this important scientific fact. Air steals away coffee flavor! All coffee ... whether ground or in the whole bean ... starts to lose flavor as soon as it's roasted, if exposed to air. In fact, ground coffee, packed in ordinary containers where air can easily reach it ... loses as much as forty-five per cent ... nearly half its precious flavor ... in only nine days.

ARNOLD: But how about Maxwell House?

HULL: Well, we think too much of this superb new Maxwell House blend to let one bit of its wonderful flavor and goodness escape. That's just why we take Maxwell House, still fresh and fragrant from the roasting ovens, and pack it in the familiar blue super-vacuum can. No air can get in … so no flavor can get out. Maxwell House comes right into your kitchen with a full measure of fresh flavor and fragrance sealed in … none wasted!

So friends … if you want coffee goodness you may never have known before … and all the goodness you've paid to enjoy, ask for Maxwell House tomorrow, won't you?

Just remember … with Maxwell House you're getting coffee that's not just days fresh, but roaster fresh! And no coffee can be fresher than that!

(MUSIC BRIDGE)

ARNOLD: We can't let the evening pass by without demanding an encore from Frank Parker. Assisted by the Maxwell House Chorus, he sings "Silver Moon" from Romberg's beautiful score of "My Maryland."

"MY MARYLAND" —PARKER, ORCHESTRA & CHORUS

(APPLAUSE)

ARNOLD: Next week, ladies and gentlemen, I want you to be with us to enjoy the performance of a charming, a beautiful, and a lovely star — Virginia Bruce—Wait until Willson hears about that. (LAUGHS) And of course we'll have Fanny Brice as Baby Snooks, with Hanley Stafford as Daddy, Bill Gargan and Benny Rubin, Connie Boswell, Meredith Willson and his orchestra — and with Virginia Bruce around, try and keep me away. So, until next Thursday, this is Edward Arnold bidding you all — goodnight.

HULL: This is Warren Hull, reminding you that leading grocers are now featuring Maxwell House Coffee at new, low prices … prices the most modest budget can afford! Now more than ever is the time to … make friends with Maxwell House!

And now … good night and good luck from the makers of Maxwell House … the coffee that's now … more than ever … Good to the Last Drop!

ANNOUNCER: This is the National Broadcasting Company.

MAXWELL HOUSE COFFEE TIME
March 26, 1942

1. SNOOKS & DADDY OPENER
2. THEME ... CAST INTRO. ... NUMBER BY CONTE
3. FRANK MORGAN SPOT
4. MIDDLE COMMERCIAL
5. ORCHESTRA NUMBER
6. BABY SNOOKS SPOT
7. CLOSING COMMERCIAL
8. THEME ... SIGNOFF
9. HITCH HIKE

(ON CUE)

BRICE:	Daddy!
FATHER:	Snooks, I'm reading.
BRICE:	You know that big puddle of water in the backyard?
FATHER:	Yes.
BRICE:	Well, Red was fishing in it.
FATHER:	Fishing? Fishing for what?
BRICE:	Squiggles.
FATHER:	Squiggles? How do you fish for squiggles?
BRICE:	With a clothes-pin, and some hamburger.
FATHER:	Ridiculous! Clothespins and hamburgers?

BRICE: It's good, daddy. You put the hamburger on the clothespin — hold it under the water — and when the squiggle bites it you snap his nose.

FATHER: I see, well, what does a squiggle look like?

BRICE: I dunno.

FATHER: You don't know?

BRICE: No — we never caught none.

FATHER: Oh. Well, go and fish some more. I want to finish my paper.

BRICE: Awight. What'll I catch, daddy?

FATHER: Catch a whale.

BRICE: With the hamburger?

FATHER: No — use a mackerel for bait.

BRICE: Why?

FATHER: Because a whale eats mackerel.

BRICE: Eats mackerel what?

FATHER: Eats Mackerel House Coffee Time. Let me read!

(THEME — APPLAUSE)

HARLOW: Translated into simple English, ladies and gentlemen, it's Maxwell House Coffee Time. And again we're happy to bring you Frank Morgan, Meredith Willson, Hanley Stafford as Daddy, and Fanny Brice as the irrepressible infant — the one and only Baby Snooks! Now, here is our master of ceremonies — your host for the evening — John Conte!

SONG — CONTE & ORCHESTRA

(APPLAUSE)

CONTE: Thank you, ladies and gentlemen — and good evening. For several weeks, as you've probably noticed, we've

	been cruising along without a guest. The reason for this is our firm policy of presenting only people who lead interesting lives — but strictly in a non-entertainment field of endeavor. Now, that type of person is hard to find.
MERE:	You mean all a fellow has to do to get on this program is not to be entertaining?
CONTE:	That's not a very complementary interpretation, Meredith — neither for the program nor our guests. However, if the shoe fits — wear it.
MERE:	What shoe?
CONTE:	Oh, no shoe. The point I'm trying to make clear in that our guests are usually in a unique profession — and have nothing whatever to do with show business.
MERE:	Oh. Well, why didn't you say so?
CONTE:	I did say so!
MERE:	You did not! You said a fellow doesn't have —
CONTE:	Go soak your pumpkin, you big bumpkin!
MERE:	Sure.
CONTE:	That's that. Ladies and gentlemen, the weather man is a person who for many years has been the butt of jokes and ridicule — but his scientific training is usually completely overlooked. Most of you are amazed to learn of the complicated preparations necessary before he can make even such a vague forecast as "Fair and cooler — with possible showers and probable rise in temperature." Of course, that's a silly example, but —
MERE:	That's not so silly, John — not for California.
CONTE:	Well it's true the weather here is rather more capricious than most other places, and that's why our weather man is a fellow who is more to be honored than scorned. So tonight I want you all to meet the

Assistant Meteorologist of the Los Angeles Weather Bureau — Harry W. Douglas. Mr. Douglas.

(APPLAUSE)

DOUGLAS: Thank you.

CONTE: I notice, Mr. Douglas, your title is Assistant Meteorologist. Why is that?

DOUGLAS: Well, I'm the acting official in charge, Mr. Conte. The chief is Merrill Bernard — but he's in Washington right now.

CONTE: Looks like he picked a good month to get out from under. How's the weather in Washington, Mr. Douglas?

DOUGLAS: Just like it is here — censored.

MERE: Jeepers! You mean you're not gonna give us a forecast for the weekend?

CONTE: He most certainly is not, Meredith!

MERE: Not even a little one?

DOUGLAS: I'm sorry, Mr. Willson, the authorities don't permit me to make public any weather prediction at all.

MERE: Well I'm not asking you for any hurricane — just tell me if it's gonna rain.

CONTE: He can't do it, Meredith. Besides, why is it so important to you?

MERE: Well, I just planted a Victory Garden and I was figuring on watering the turnips tomorrow — but if it's gonna rain I could save around —

CONTE: Meredith! Are you insane?

MERE: Sure. What do you mean?

CONTE: You want this man to divulge information that may be vital to the enemy just to save you an eighteen-cent water bill?

MERE:	I never thought of that. Well — I tell you what, Mr. Douglas — you just tell me privately — and then I can tell my Jap gardener.
CONTE:	Why don't you just wire it to the Tokyo Times?
MERE:	Well, I —
CONTE:	Please let me interview Mr. Douglas, will you, Meredith?
MERE:	Sure. (MUMBLES) Never heard such a fuss over a little hunk of weather. Bet he don't know himself. Hmmm.
CONTE:	Keep quiet! Mr. Douglas, how does the weather man arrive at a forecast?
DOUGLAS:	Well, we use a weather map which is plotted from the data we receive from our observers. Here's one you can look at.
CONTE:	Say, that's wonderful. Are you sure it's all right for me to see it?
DOUGLAS:	I think so - it happens to be last week's.
CONTE:	I see. What are all these crayon marks?
DOUGLAS:	They indicate the warm fronts and cold fronts. There's the high pressure area — and there's the low. Those black, concentric ovals are called isobars.
CONTE:	Very complex. Is this your forecast written at the bottom?
DOUGLAS:	That's it.
CONTE:	Big wind approaching!
MORGAN:	(COMING) I heard that, Jockey — and it's a dastardly way to announce my entrance!
CONTE:	Frank!
	(APPLAUSE)

MORGAN:	I won't have you kicking me in the face when my back is turned! Why is it I can't —
CONTE:	Frank! I wasn't announcing your entrance — I was talking about another big wind!
MORGAN:	Oh, another one. What?
MERE:	We're just discussing the weather, Frank.
MORGAN:	Oh — the weather. Well, I can see your conversation is rapidly progressing upward to the level of idiots. Soon I'll walk in here and find you — oh, hello, Meredith.
MERE:	Hello.
MORGAN:	Let's have a look at you. May I say your appearance fascinates me?
MERE:	Pray do.
MORGAN:	You have the spruce look of a well-tubbed goat-herder, who polishes your nose?
MERE:	Nobody, Frank. I just scrub my whole face with a sink brush.
MORGAN:	Well, keep it up, my boy — I've heard it said that constant scrubbing will wear away even a stone. You may go.
MERE:	Thank you. (HE GOES)
CONTE:	Now, that's what I call a real intelligent conversation — it makes our weather discussion sound like a thesis on semantics.
MORGAN:	Well, let's leave religion out of this. What brought about this uncommon topic of the weather?
CONTE:	I just happened to glance at this gentleman's map. It's unbelievable.
MORGAN:	Yes, I thought his map was rather ghastly myself — but I was too polite to say so. Still I don't unders——

CONTE: It's a weather map, sap!

MORGAN: Oh, mapsap. Weather!

CONTE: From the Los Angeles Weather Bureau. You can look at it if you think it'll make any sense to you. Here.

MORGAN: Hmmm. Very interesting. (TO HIMSELF) Low pressure area latitude 45 North, longitude 135 East.. Polar easterly on semipermanent Pacific High ... Hmmm ... (BEGINS TO ENJOY IT) Whirling storm temperate zone.. (MUMBLES AND LAUGHS) ..rising barometric pressure. Very interesting.

CONTE: Wait a minute! Are you trying to make us believe you understand that weather mar, Morgan?

MORGAN: (LAUGHS) Are you serious, Jockey? Would you ask Sir Christopher Wren if he understood the plans of St. Paul's?

CONTE: But he drew those plans!

MORGAN: Well?

CONTE: Oh, no!

MORGAN: Oh yes!

DOUGLAS: Excuse me, Mr. Morgan —

MORGAN: What is it, laddie-buck?

DOUGLAS: That map came from the Los Angeles Weather Station, and —

MORGAN: I know where it came from, son! And we call it the Meteorological Bureau. Of course, you wouldn't understand those technical terms —

CONTE: Frank!

MORGAN: Jockey, will tell your son here, to —

CONTE: He's not my son!

MORGAN: He's not?

DOUGLAS: No, I'm not!

MORGAN: Well, you both have my congratulations. But this is one of my own maps, issued since I took charge of the Bureau as Chief Meteorologist. If you demand further proof, witness the initials F.M. in the left-hand corner of the map.

CONTE: There it is — F.M. What the —

MORGAN: (PATRONIZINGLY) I don't suppose I have to tell you what F.M. stands for, gentlemen.

DOUGLAS: No — it stands for Full Moon.

MORGAN: Oh — err — full moon. Well, when the moon is full so is Morgan — so they're practically synonymous. (GIGGLES) (That's the weakest crawl-out I've had in ten years.) Well, I have to —

CONTE: Hold it! What's this wet hay about being the Chief Meteorologist, Frank?

DOUGLAS: Yes. The Chief of the Bureau is Mr. Bernard, he came from Saint Louis.

MORGAN: Oh — Saint Bernard. Err —

CONTE: Yes — and he happens to be in Washington right now.

MORGAN: Moves around, doesn't he? Do you know why he happens to be in Washington?

CONTE: Er — do you?

DOUGLAS: Frankly, I don't.

MORGAN: (RELIEVED) Well, the coast is clear — and that's not a weather report! I don't like to wash any dirty linen in public — but if you'll keep it mum I'll tell you why I replaced him.

CONTE: Replaced him?

MORGAN: Yes. The Central Bureau in Washington got fed up with the unreliable weather reports from here, and in these critical times accuracy is the byword. My record as a weather expert meteorologist left the government only one course — of course —

CONTE: Of course —

MORGAN: Of course. It's true another climatic expert was being considered for the important post, a man highly proficient in snow conditions —

CONTE: In California.

MORGAN: Precisely. But my uncanny forecasts of impending hail swayed the board and they turned down the man with the snow.

DOUGLAS: And they took you.

MORGAN: Yes — their decision was the hail with Morgan. (I'm afraid there's a leak in the Bureau, fellows.)

CONTE: Okay, Frank. So now you're in complete charge. You have an assistant meteorologist working with you, I presume?

MORGAN: He's with me — but he doesn't work, Jockey.

CONTE: I see. And your assistant would be a certain Mr. Harry W. Douglas, would it not?

MORGAN: It would? I mean it would! Douglas — yes, that's the loafer's name. I'm getting rid of him this week, though.

DOUGLAS: Well, this comes as a great shock to me, Mr. Morgan.

MORGAN: It wouldn't be a shock, sir, if you knew this Douglas. A more thoroughly inefficient lout never bribed his way thru a Civil Service examination! Light-fingered, too!

DOUGLAS: What!

MORGAN: Yes. That's why I'm discharging him — a little matter of stealing postage stamps.

CONTE: Did you catch him stealing the stamps, Frank?

MORGAN: No, but he certainly mails a lot of letters for a fellow who has no friends. I might even have overlooked that if he had the slightest idea of how to make a forecast.

DOUGLAS: You mean this — this —

MORGAN: Faker.

DOUGLAS: This faker, Douglas, doesn't know anything about meteorology?

MORGAN: Well, I'd be willing to wager he knows even less about it than you do — if such a thing is possible. And when I look at you, anything's possible!

CONTE: Wonderful world!

MORGAN: Just imagine, gentlemen, when I first entered the Bureau as Chief, I instructed my half-witted assistant —

CONTE: Douglas.

MORGAN: Yes, Douglas! I instructed him to take hourly readings of the anemometer and hygrometer, and report —

CONTE: What's an anemometer and a hygrometer?

MORGAN: Well — err —

DOUGLAS: An anemometer is used to determine wind velocity, and a hygrometer measures moisture in the air.

MORGAN: Yes. I told — you know something about meteorology, son?

DOUGLAS: About as much as Douglas.

MORGAN: Oh. You had me nervous for a minute. Well, it didn't take me long to find out this chap was unable to check his wind and water. Then I gave him every instrument at our disposal, including a theodolite and several radiosondes, and asked him to make a complete forecast.

CONTE:	And?
MORGAN:	I watched him surreptitiously as he fumbled with the instruments — obviously he knew nothing about them —
DOUGLAS:	Yes?
MORGAN:	But oddly enough, when he predicted rain — it rained!
CONTE:	Why was that?
MORGAN:	I found out he was depending on a corn on his left big toe! Well, I can't stand to talk about the man's incompetence anymore, so I'll —
CONTE:	Don't run, Frank. Wouldn't you like to know who this gentleman is?
MORGAN:	Jockey, I've told you time and again, your ignorant friends don't inter—oh! I — feel a storm brewing. Don't tell me this is —
CONTE:	Yes. You'll be glad to know this is Harry W. Douglas — assistant meteorologist of the Los Angeles Weather Bureau!
MORGAN:	Oh — meteor — glad. Glad to meteor. See you again. Well —
CONTE:	No, you don't! First you apologize to Mr. Douglas for all of your slurring remarks about him!
MORGAN:	Take your grubby hands off of me, Grubby!
CONTE:	Apologize!
MORGAN:	You can't make — I mean, I didn't know — nobody showed me the script before — why should I — Meredith?
MERE:	Right here, Frank!
MORGAN:	What are you waiting for, you oaf!

MERE:	(TREMULOUSLY) Mr. Douglas, I'm sorry for anything nasty that was said about you and I'm to blame for the whole thing. Is that all right, Frank?
MORGAN:	No — it's too fawning. Go away. Mr. Douglas, if you accept that kind of an apology I'll lose whatever respect I'm trying vainly to muster for you.
DOUGLAS:	Oh, that's all right, Mr. Morgan. I forgive Mr. Willson for everything you said.
CONTE:	The place is a madhouse! Then you admit, Frank, the whole meteorology business was something you just dreamed up?
MORGAN:	My dreams are none of your concern, Concert! I may have erred slightly in claiming to be the Chief Meteorologist in Los Angeles — but my record still stands.
CONTE:	Where do you get the gall? You know this man can nail you if you start to lie about his profession!
MORGAN:	Since when do I lie — don't answer that! Besides, you've just heard testimony that Mr. Douglas is thoroughly incompetent in — what am I saying?
DOUGLAS:	Mr. Morgan, it's apparent to me that you must have some knowledge of meteorology. I could tell by the way you read that weather map.
MORGAN:	There! That proves he knows less than I think he does. You're a man of sound judgment, Mr. Douglas. Some day I'll tell you of the history of the Morgan family as weather prophets.
CONTE:	Tell us now.
MORGAN:	Very well. It all began with my grandfather, Drizzle Morgan —
CONTE:	Drizzle Morgan. Frank, since you've been on this program you've had thirty-seven grandfathers — I've been keeping track of them.

MORGAN: You have? Well, that's more than my grandmother did. (GIGGLES) But old Drizzle was one of the few strangely endowed humans known as rainmakers.

DOUGLAS: Oh, yes.

MORGAN: Oh, yes, he says. His services were in demand to produce rain from Maine to California, and my old gaffer was never found in a dry state. That's a gift we all inherited. (Hmm — I think there's a double meaning there.)

CONTE: If there is I only got one of them. How did your gaffer go about making rain, Barrel?

MORGAN: Oh, rain barrel. Well, for many years he worked secretly on a device employing a principle used centuries before by the Zulu pygmies. His tools were crude and undeveloped, but he had a brain to match them. And he remained undismayed by his first nine hundred failures. It wasn't until seven years after he started that the world became aware of his secret vice. Device!

CONTE: Perseverance wins.

MORGAN: It would appear so. As luck would have it, the state of Kansas was suffering the worst drought in history, and my gaffer made the trek on foot, hugging along his huge rainmaking machine.

DOUGLAS: Where did he live?

MORGAN: In Kansas. The drought was killing livestock and crops and ruining farms and homesteads -

CONTE: Must have been pretty dry.

MORGAN: Dry! They had bullfrogs there over six years old who'd never learned to swim. But this didn't bother old Drizzle. He set up his machine in a deserted barn, locked himself from the prying eyes of the skeptical farmers, whom he had charged a dollar a piece and promised them, rain within twenty-four hours!

CONTE:	Meredith — quick!
MERE:	(RUSHES IN) Okay. Gee, this is interesting. What was it?
MORGAN:	Go away!
MERE:	Sure.
MORGAN:	As the hours ticked slowly by, the crowd outside the barn became larger and more restive. Still the sun beat down with fierce gloating. The truculent people began arming themselves with clubs and rocks, to present to my gaffer should he fail.
DOUGLAS:	Well?
MORGAN:	Two minutes before the twenty-fourth hour the skies grew leaden — clouds began to form —
CONTE:	Uh-huh.
MORGAN:	As the last second struck — a huge farmer electrified the crowd by declaring he'd caught a drip!
CONTE:	It was rain!
MORGAN:	No — it was my grandfather — he was trying to sneak out the back door. Well so long, fellows, I gotta buy an umbrella.
	(MUSIC ... APPLAUSE)
	MIDDLE COMMERCIAL
SOUND:	(TWIN-MOTORED PLANE WARMING UP FOR TAKE-OFF ... HOLD)
MERE:	(AGAINST SOUND) Gosh ... sounds like an airport.
CONTE:	It is, Meredith. We're about to take off on a fancied flight.
MERE:	Suits me — fancy or otherwise. Where to, John?
CONTE:	Well, you try to guess from the tips I give.

MORGAN: *You* give tips, Jockey? I've got to see *this*. I'm going along.

CONTE: Okay, Frank. Here we go! (MOTORS UP TO FLIGHT SPEED ... HOLD AS B.G.) First tip and first stop ... via Pan American Airways to Balboa.

MERE: I know ... that's in Panama!

MORGAN: And then south by Pan American-Grace Airways! Never shall I forget the first plane I flew over the Panagra Route ... only I flew it *backwards*.

CONTE: What ... the plane?

MORGAN: No, the route. From Buenos Aires northwest to Santiago, then north to Antofagasta, La Paz, Lima ... marvelous country!

CONTE: For once you know what you're talking about, Frank. Except you didn't pilot the plane!

MORGAN: Well ... not clear up to the Canal Zone. I left my passengers at Cali, Colombia ... (PLANE LANDS, CUT MOTORS) ... then hurried over to transact some business at Bogata and Medellin.

(START COMMERCIAL TIME HERE ... 225 WORDS, 1 MINUTE, 17 SECONDS)

MIDDLE COMMERCIAL (CONT.)

MERE: Exploring Inca ruins, I presume?

CONTE: No, Meredith. You see, it was lunch time and the steward ran out of coffee. So Frank slipped over to replenish the supply with more of the same extra-flavor, highland-grown coffees ...

MORGAN: (SURPRISED) Why, Conte, how did you know it was the *same*?

CONTE: Easy, Frank. I knew Pan American serves *Maxwell House Coffee*!

WILCOX: And the superb Maxwell House blend contains an *extra* measure of premium Medellins for richness ... Manizales for mellowness ... Bucaramangas for full body ... Central and South Americans for vigorous, winy flavor.

CONTE: Yes — and people who fly over Colombia can look down on those famous coffee groves nestled in the sun-drenched uplands ... and then enjoy the rare qualities each coffee contributes to the Maxwell House they drink aloft.

WILCOX: Top-grade coffees such as these — picked at the peak of ripe perfection — naturally cost more to buy. Yet cup for cup, Maxwell House costs you but a *fraction* of a penny more than the cheapest coffees sold!

So it's now wonder that, today, Maxwell House is the largest-selling vacuum-packed coffee in the world ... and has been chosen for the discriminating travelers who are passengers on the Clippers of Pan American Airways System.

Try Maxwell House, won't you? Enjoy the savor, freshness and flavor of the coffee that's *now* — more than ever ... *Good* to the Last Drop!

CONTE: Swell, Meredith. And now, ladies and — (PHONE RINGS)

CONTE: Excuse me. Hello.

STAFF: (FILTER ... GUARDED) John?

CONTE: Yes, daddy?

STAFF: I'll be a little late for the poker game tonight.

CONTE: Where are you going?

STAFF: Well, I joined the first aid squad in our district, and I have to take my Red Cross exam tonight.

CONTE: You mean you've been taking instructions for several weeks?

STAFF:	Every Thursday. Well, I'll see you later.
CONTE:	I hope you pass, daddy.
STAFF:	Thanks. So long.
CONTE:	Goodbye. (HANGS UP) Poor, daddy — he'll do anything to get out of the house!
	(SNOOKS PLAY-ON)
FATHER:	Well, I guess she's asleep now. She's been quiet for three minutes. Where's my hat?
BRICE:	Here it is, daddy.
FATHER:	Snooks! Didn't you promise me you wouldn't leave your bed tonight?
BRICE:	Uh-huh.
FATHER:	And didn't I promise to spank you if you did?
BRICE:	Uh-huh.
FATHER:	Well!
BRICE:	Well, I didn't keep my promise — so you needn't keep yours, daddy.
FATHER:	All right. I won't spank you if you go back to bed right now.
BRICE:	Why?
FATHER:	Why? Must we go thru this every night?
BRICE:	Yeah — every night.
FATHER:	Well, I'm tired of it. I put you to bed and you hop out again. In again — out again!
BRICE:	I'm like a rubber ball, ain't I?
FATHER:	Yes!
BRICE:	You wanna see me bounce on my —

FATHER: No — I don't want to see you bounce on your head!

BRICE: I wasn't gonna say my —

FATHER: I don't care! Now, don't make me yell at you. I have to be very calm this evening.

BRICE: Why?

FATHER: I'm going to take my Red Cross examination. I'm studying first aid.

BRICE: Can you drink it?

FATHER: Why should you drink first aid?

BRICE: Ain't it like lemonade?

FATHER: (MIMICS HER) No, it ain't like lemonade! First aid is the immediate, temporary treatment given in case of accident or sudden illness before the services of a physician can be secured. Now, I have to go.

BRICE: Where's the accident, daddy?

FATHER: There isn't any accident.

BRICE: Then where are you going?

FATHER: To take my examination. I've been studying the stuff for six weeks.

BRICE: What stuff?

FATHER: First aid! Will you please go to bed, Snooks?

BRICE: No.

FATHER: Why not?

BRICE: I wanna see the accident.

FATHER: Snooks!

BRICE: I wanna see the accident!

FATHER:	Stop that! I told you there wasn't any accident. I'm just learning what to do in case there is an accident.
BRICE:	Make one and let me see.
FATHER:	What's the matter with you?
BRICE:	Let's conk Robespierre with a baseball bat!
FATHER:	You bloodthirsty little heathen! Conk Robespierre with a baseball bat!
BRICE:	Yeah — conk him.
FATHER:	Don't you ever express such wicked thoughts again as long as you live! Conk Robespierre!
BRICE:	Shall we conk mummy?
FATHER:	We won't conk anyb— Hmmmm.
BRICE:	Shall we?
FATHER:	Now you're going from the ridiculous to the sublime. I won't be an accessory to any of your conking parties — but what you do after I leave is your own business. Goodnight.
BRICE:	Goodnight, Daddy ... Daddy?
FATHER:	Yes?
BRICE:	Where are you going?
FATHER:	I told you I'm going to a meeting of the Red Cross, didn't I?
BRICE:	Yeah, that's what you told me, all right.
FATHER:	Well?
BRICE:	Well, I wanna know where you're going.
FATHER:	To a meeting of the Red Cross! I'm going to take my first aid examination!

BRICE: Why?

FATHER: Because I am! Why do I stand here and let you cross-examine me?

BRICE: Because it's a Red Cross examination.

FATHER: Very funny — very funny. (NASTY LAUGH)

BRICE: (LAUGHS) Waaaaahhhh!

FATHER: Oh, keep quiet and go to bed. Please, Snooks — I don't want to be late for this thing. If I miss it I'll have to take the course all over again.

BRICE: What do you have to do, daddy?

FATHER: It's almost like being a doctor.

BRICE: Is that why you're carrying that black bag?

FATHER: Yes, of course.

BRICE: Show me the baby.

FATHER: Baby?

BRICE: Yeah — in the bag.

FATHER: There isn't any baby in the bag, silly.

BRICE: Well, every time the doctor goes to Aunt Sophie with his black bag he bring another —

FATHER: Oh, nonsense. This bag contains bandages, splints, tape and stuff like that. It's just an emergency kit.

BRICE: Well, I wanna see him.

FATHER: See who?

BRICE: The kid.

FATHER: Kit — not kid! Here — look in the bag. Go ahead.

BRICE: Awight … what's this wood for, daddy?

FATHER:	Those are splints. We use those whenever there's a fracture. That means a broken bone. Do you have any idea how many bones there are inside of you?
BRICE:	You mean from those sardines I ate?
FATHER:	No, your own bones. Take your spine for instance — that bony thing that runs down your back.
BRICE:	Is it running, daddy?
FATHER:	No — you can feel it. Right there. That's your spinal column. Your head sits on one end —
BRICE:	And I sit on the other.
FATHER:	Exactly. In your spine alone there are a great many bones called vertebrae.
BRICE:	How many?
FATHER:	Ahh — see! If I hadn't studied first aid I'd never know the answer to that.
BRICE:	Well, how many is there?
FATHER:	Well, there's seven cervical, twelve thoracic, err — six — no, eight lumbar, I think — and er — the sacral, well — just take the leg.
BRICE:	What about the spine?
FATHER:	It doesn't really matter — if you break that you're finished anyhow.
BRICE:	Good thing you know the answers, ain't it, daddy?
FATHER:	I better have another look at that text-book. Here, Snooks — take the book and ask me some of the questions.
BRICE:	Awight. Where shall I start?
FATHER:	Start on the bones of the head. I think it's on page eleven. See it there — the cranium?

BRICE:	No. All I see is a man with his outside off and his inside sticking out.
FATHER:	That's a skeleton. You have one of those inside of you.
BRICE:	Huh?
FATHER:	Sure. So have I — so has mummy — and Robespierre. We all have those things inside of us.
BRICE:	We're a wonderful family, ain't we, daddy?
FATHER:	Wonderful. Hurry up — call out a few questions. Have you got the bones of the head? You've got it — right there. Start with the maxilla.
BRICE:	What?
FATHER:	Maxilla?
BRICE:	Maxilla House Coffee Time?
FATHER:	No — maxilla! Jawbone! Don't you remember the story about Samson?
BRICE:	Samson who?
FATHER:	Samson! The strong man — the one who slew a thousand Philistines.
BRICE:	Oh, yeah.
FATHER:	How did he slay them?
BRICE:	I dunno.
FATHER:	You do too. With — with — (INDICATES JAW) — what am I pointing to?
BRICE:	Oh, I know. The jawbone of an ass.
FATHER:	That's right.
BRICE:	I wouldn't remember it if you didn't point to your face, daddy.
FATHER:	Fine. Well — come on — ask me some questions!

FATHER:	Awight. How many bones in the face?
FATHER:	That's easy — nine.
BRICE:	Nine?
FATHER:	Certainly.
BRICE:	The book is wrong, daddy — it says fourteen.
FATHER:	Huh? Let me see — I'll be hanged! Must be a misprint. Let's skip the bones for awhile. Ask me anything else.
BRICE:	Here's a good done. (READS) If a man is suffering from a hemstitcher —
FATHER:	Hemorrhage!
BRICE:	Yeah. How do you cut off his blonde supply?
FATHER:	Blonde supply! You can't even read — that's blood supply.
BRICE:	Well, how do you cut it off?
FATHER:	With a tourniquet. Next? Hurry up — I don't want to be late for that exam.
BRICE:	If a woman's back is very sunburned — what do you do?
FATHER:	A woman, huh?
BRICE:	Yeah, a woman.
FATHER:	Sunburned back. Hmm. Can't think — what do you do if a woman burns her back?
BRICE:	It says turn over.
FATHER:	They mean turn the page!
BRICE:	Oh, just a second, daddy. Here it is. Roll her over a barrel and pull her tongue out and tie it to —
FATHER:	You've skipped two pages. That's the chapter on drowning — and it says never to roll a person on a barrel!

BRICE: Well, you ask me the questions.

FATHER: No, I've go to leave. Give me my bag.

BRICE: Take me with you, daddy.

FATHER: No! What do you want to go for?

BRICE: I like accidents!

FATHER: Don't talk like that. There's nothing more unpleasant than an accident. You remember how awful it was when mummy got bitten by that mad dog.

BRICE: Was that an accident, daddy?

FATHER: Sure it was.

BRICE: I thought he done it on purpose.

FATHER: Nonsense — the animal didn't even know mummy. Well, goodnight, Snooks.

BRICE: No, don't go, daddy.

FATHER: I must go! They're waiting for me to pass my bandaging test — a man's going to act as a patient.

BRICE: Try it on me, first.

FATHER: I haven't got the — (AN IDEA) … Oh. All right, Snooks. Hop into bed.

BRICE: Awight.

FATHER: Now, put your hands together — and lie flat. Watch how fast I bandage you … Now give me your feet.

BRICE: Together?

FATHER: Yes … This is called the cravat bandage — tell me if it's too tight.

BRICE: I like it.

FATHER: Fine. Now — one big bandage — right around your body —

BRICE:	What are you trying it around the bed for, daddy?
FATHER:	Now, some tape across your mouth —
BRICE:	(MUMBLES)
FATHER:	Can you move, Snooks?
BRICE:	(MUMBLES)
FATHER:	Fine. Goodnight!
BRICE:	Waaaaahhhhhh!

(MUSIC ... APPLAUSE)

CLOSING COMMERCIAL
(193 WORDS — 1 MIN 6 SECS)

BRICE:	Da-a-addy.
FATHER:	Yes, Snooks.
BRICE:	(CONFIDENTIALLY) Me an' Mommy *seen* 'em.
FATHER:	No. Mommy and *I saw* them.
BRICE:	Didja? *Nice*, ain't they?
FATHER:	(YELLS) How do I know? What *are* they?
CONTE:	(YELLS RIGHT BACK) *The new Duraglas vacuum jars of Maxwell House Coffee!* (NORMALLY) And ladies, *you'll* see them at your grocer's, too ... for they represent Maxwell House Coffee's adjustment to all-out war requirements.
WILCOX:	Yes, we have perfected in Duraglas the *same* super-vacuum pack that's *always* protected Maxwell House ... the one way science knows to bring you perfect coffee, *roaster*-fresh!
	Now it's vacuum-packed *two* ways. No difference whatever between them — they're *both the same*. And both may be available for a time at some stores ... while others may carry Maxwell House only in glass, or only

in cans. We can't tell exactly, because there's no way to know what our country's future needs may be.

But rest assured! Whether you buy the glass or the can ... whether you use Drip, Regular, or Glass-Maker Grind ... you get *identically* the same roaster-fresh Maxwell House — with *precisely* the same super-vacuum protection at no extra cost to you!

Tomorrow, buy Maxwell House Coffee ... vacuum-packed *two* ways ... roaster-fresh *always*!

(THEME — FADING FOR)

CONTE: Well, that's about all the time we have, ladies and gentlemen, but we'll be back again next Thursday evening at Maxwell House Coffee Time ... Fanny Brice as Baby Snooks, Frank Morgan, who appears with us through the courtesy of Metro-Goldwyn-Mayer, Hanley Stafford, Meredith Willson and his orchestra, and Harlow Wilcox.

Maxwell House Coffee Time is written by Phil Rapp.

Until next Thursday then, this is John Conte saying goodnight and good luck from the makers of Maxwell House ... the coffee that is always ... good to the last drop!

BINGMAN: When you're feeling like a hermit
And on gloomy thoughts you dwell
Heed advice that wise men offer
"Life is swell when you keep well!" (SMILES) Friends ... you'll *want* to get out and have fun ... when you feel fit! So start each day with Post's Forty Per Cent Bran Flakes — the delicious bran flake cereal that supplies three wonderful "Keep fit" benefits! Wheat for nourishment ... enough extra bran for bulk ... added Vitamin B-1 for energy!

Order Post's Bran Flakes *tomorrow*!

This is the National Broadcasting Company.

MAXWELL HOUSE COFFEE TIME
June 19, 1941

1. SNOOKS AND DADDY
2. THEME AND CAST INTRODUCTION "LONG ABOUT SUNDOWN"
3. FRANK MORGAN
4. COMMERCIAL
5. "DREAM OF LOVE"
6. BABY SNOOKS
7. COMMERCIAL
8. "THE RELUCTANT DRAGON"
9. SIGN-OFF
10. HITCH-HIKE

CONTE: Frank!

(APPLAUSE)

MORGAN: Hello, fellows. Let's see that telegram, son.

CONTE: It's not for you, Frank. It's for Hanley Stafford.

MORGAN: Hanley Stafford! That incompetent, conceited, child-beating …

STAFFORD: Oh, now just a minute, Frank! Is that a nice thing to say?

MORGAN: Better than he deserves! Oh, hello, Meredith. Can you imagine anybody … when did you raise that mustache, Meredith?

STAFFORD: Meredith? I'm Stafford.

MORGAN:	Well, my dear boy, it's not necessary to tell me who— STAFFORD! This is a plot! Where's my parachute? I'm going to Scotland!
CONTE:	Take it easy, Frank. And try to be a little more topical with your crawl-outs.
MORGAN:	Oh — tropical louts. Well, I—
STAFFORD:	I'm sure you didn't mean anything, Frank. Don't apologize. I'll be running along now—see you later, John. (HE BUNGS OFF)
CONTE:	So long, Daddy.
MORGAN:	So long.
CONTE:	Now, Frank—what prompted that nasty outburst against a nice fellow like Hanley?
MORGAN:	Nasty outburst? Why, he's one of the most charming, self-effacing—is he gone?
CONTE:	He's gone.
MORGAN:	That conniving weasel! You'll do well to stay clear of that loose fish, my boy—he's an ugly customer!
MEREDITH:	What's this? What's this?
MORGAN:	Oh, hello, Meredith. You are Meredith, aren't you?
MEREDITH:	Sure. What's the matter, Frank?
MORGAN:	I had the misfortune to allow Stafford to inveigle me in a card game last night—
CONTE:	Card game?
MORGAN:	I'm referring to the new card game called gin, rummy. I mean gin-rummy. My suspicions were aroused when he insisted on using his own cards, and when he stationed that fearsome child of his behind me I knew I was being fleeced.
MEREDITH:	Well, shear my wool and call me mutton!

MORGAN:	Yes. Through an elaborate set of signals, Stafford was made aware of the cards I held and it was only by canny playing and a lightning switch to my own marked deck that I was able to beat him out of twelve dollars. But that's the last time I'll play cards with a cheat!
CONTE:	I suppose you've never played with a cheat before?
MORGAN:	Only when I play solitaire. Who said that!
CONTE:	Frank, I refuse to believe that Hanley and Snooks would try to cheat you out of any money, and what's more, I don't believe that even you would stoop so low as to use a marked deck of cards!
MEREDITH:	Well, I believe it! Go on, Frank!
MORGAN:	Thank you, Meredith. Your loyalty has now reached such a stage of revulsion that I feel compelled to dispense with your friendship!
MEREDITH:	(PROUD) How's that, huh, John? Huh? John, huh? How's that, boy?
CONTE:	What's the matter with you! Morgan's giving you the brush!
MEREDITH:	Don't try to start trouble between old friends, Conte! Never mind what he says, Frank, I'm with you! I'll stick to you like glue!
MORGAN:	The feeling is mucilage. (Well, I can see we're getting near the end of the season now.) So long, boys, I'm—
SOUND:	(PHONE RINGS)
CONTE:	Wait a second, Frank ... Hello.
MAN:	(FILTER) Listen, Morgan—this is Fred the bookmaker. I just heard you say you beat a guy out of twelve bucks last night—
CONTE:	Just a—
MAN:	(FILTER) Now, don't stall! You owe me eleven dollars

	from Tuesday's races — and five dollars you lost on the fight last night. I want my sixteen dollars and I want it quick!
CONTE:	Well, stop yelling! This is not Morgan, but I'll put him on. For you, Frank.
MORGAN:	Oh ... hello.
MAN:	Hello. This is Fred the bookmaker. I want my sixteen dollars, Morgan.
MORGAN:	Oh—er—you—yes. Well, you'll have to call me at home. I can't talk about insurance today. Good morning.
MAN:	(HOLLERS) Good morning my foot! I want my sixteen bucks!
MORGAN:	No, I think the two hundred thousand dollar annuity would be safest for me. I'll pay it in one premium.
MAN:	What premium! I want my sixteen bucks!
MEREDITH:	Jeepers! Do you let your insurance man holler at you like that, Frank?
MORGAN:	That's my policy. (GIGGLES) Hello, Mr. Snarley — you just notify the New York Life that I'll —
MAN:	Will you stop with that crazy talk! I gotta have my dough!
MORGAN:	Very well. Stop by the house tonight and I'll give you a check. (HANGS UP) Fred's a fine insurance salesman, but a bit on the high-pressure side—for a low-life.
CONTE:	Mmm-hmm. Since when does the New York Life take bets on horses, Frank?
MORGAN:	Err—horses Frank ... New York beds ... err—did—he say anything to you about betting, Concord?
CONTE:	He said he was your bookmaker, faker!

MORGAN:	Well, it's true. I don't make very many wagers, but I couldn't pass up a good thing like last night's boxing match, and with the inside information I managed to procure, I cleaned up eighty thousand dollars.
MEREDITH:	Gee, this is interesting. (BIG) Eighty thousand dollars!
MORGAN:	Yes, my son. Whenever I make a bet it's a sure thing! Gamblers come from miles around to pry out my precious predictions prior to prizefights.
CONTE:	Uh-huh.
MORGAN:	My tips never fail and it's a common saying among the betting world—wherever Morgan is you'll find the dope! (How many more have we got, fellows?)
CONTE:	Never mind that, Frank. Where do you get the gall to say you won eighty thousand dollars, when the guy just said it was five dollars—and you lost it!
MORGAN:	Must I stand here and be cross-examined by a—
CONTE:	Well, it's true, isn't it?
MORGAN:	I refuse to be shaken up and down by the forward remarks of a backward underling! (GIGGLES) That's a pretty good aside!
MEREDITH:	Top that, Johnny boy! If Frank says he won eighty thousand, he won eighty thousand dollars! Go on, Frank!
MORGAN:	Oh, dear. Well, I can assure you that winning a paltry eighty thousand dollars is not a thrill for a man who broke the bank at Monte Carlo seven times!
CONTE:	Oh, this is going too far!
MORGAN:	I think so, too—but I'm into it now!
MEREDITH:	What are you talking about? Didn't you break the bank at Monte Carlo, Frank?
CONTE:	Tell him, Morgan!

MORGAN: Roulette Morgan, sir! For generations the Morgan family has busted the bank, and I'm the last of a long line of busts! Busters!

MEREDITH: Oh boy, I love this!

MORGAN: The gaming interests at Monaco quake in their shoes whenever a Morgan approaches the famous casino — dating back to the days when my Uncle Bluechip Morgan first devised a system for beating the wheel!

CONTE: What was the system?

MORGAN: Have you ever heard of the Fisticuff system of arithmetical progression?

CONTE: No.

MEREDITH: Me neither, Frank.

MORGAN: That makes three of us. But it's infallible. Adapted by my Uncle Bluechip it runs as follows. Wait until red shows on the wheel, then play black three times in a row, doubling your stakes. Switch to red twice, then back to black until you reach the fifteenth level, then you divide by four and start at one. If it still leaks put a pan under it and we'll have a man right over. (What is that?)

CONTE: And your Uncle won with that system?

MORGAN: Every single night he won fifty dollars. There was only one hitch.

MEREDITH: What was that?

MORGAN: It was costing him a thousand dollars a day to live. A mere detail, but important enough to convince the family that Uncle Bluechip should be committed at once to a mental institution.

CONTE: A smart apple, Uncle Bluechip.

MORGAN: De mortuis nil nisi bonum. But my mathematical eye

	and the law of averages convinced me the system would work with a little rearranging. So on the ninth of June, 1921, I left for the French Riviera, armed with a huge bankroll and the new system.
MEREDITH:	Did you go right to Monte Carlo, Frank?
MORGAN:	No. I spent many months in Europe testing the system, and first began to show a profit at a famous gambling house in Haida-Pasha, which lies in a remote corner of Turkey.
CONTE:	You wanted to make sure, eh?
MORGAN:	I was using the utmost caution. But my plans almost went awry when I reached the Kirmantash Province, and—
CONTE:	Kirmantash Province? What's that?
MORGAN:	Another portion of Turkey.
CONTE:	Cranberry sauce?
MORGAN:	Just gravy, if you pl—what are we talking about!
MEREDITH:	Cut it out, John! Go on, Frank! What happened to your plans?
MORGAN:	Well, as usual I carried a large sum of currency in my pocket, and I had to traverse many dark alleys to reach the gaming room. As I rounded one corner, a slim figure slipped from the shadows and leveled a pistol at me.
CONTE:	A Turkish stick-up.
MORGAN:	Exactly. I sparred for time, and as my eyes became accustomed to the darkness, I could make out the form of the footpad. It was a woman!
MEREDITH:	Wow!
MORGAN:	Yes. (GIGGLES) It didn't take me long to convince her she was in the wrong profession, and after a bit of a—shall we say lecture—I let her go.

CONTE:	Did you take her pistol away?
MORGAN:	Certainly. And to assure myself she had no more weapons I gave her a superficial frisking — in a thorough sort of way. That night I left for France, reached the Riviera, and rented a villa.
CONTE:	By the sea?
MORGAN:	No, by the week. I wish you boys could have seen the mansion! The furniture was positively regal! Downstairs, Louis the Fourteenth, upstairs, Louis the Fifteenth, and in the attic, Louis Jambon.
CONTE:	Louis Jambon?
MORGAN:	The caretaker's brother. He lived up there with a goat. (SHAKES HIS HEAD) The whole thing is mad.
MEREDITH:	Who cares! Hurry up and break the bank, Frank!
MORGAN:	Have patience, my son. I remained closeted in my villa for three weeks, working on my system day and night. Then I engaged a beautiful female croupier, and practiced calling the sections as she spun the wheel.
CONTE:	Did you get her number?
MORGAN:	She didn't have a phone, but I managed to—oh! You mean number on the wheel! Certainly—every time. I knew my moment had arrived.
MEREDITH:	Oh, boy!
MORGAN:	One night about ten o'clock, the blasé hangers-on of Monte Carlo sat up in their chairs as a handsome, faultlessly tailored young man, with the Legion D'Honneur across his shirt front, strode into the Casino! Inside of two hours, he had won three billion francs and broken the bank!
MEREDITH:	It was you!
MORGAN:	No, I was at the next table and lost a dollar sixty. Well, so long, fellows—I gotta buy a Racing Form!

(MUSIC ... APPLAUSE)

COMMERCIAL
MIDDLE—284 WORDS-1 MINUTE 39 SECONDS

CONTE: Meredith, if I gave you a big piece of pie ... *fresh* from the oven ... *fragrant* with the aroma of tender, juicy apples ... *topped* with a flaky crust of golden brown ... *what would you say?*

MEREDITH: Why, I'd say ... where's the coffee?

CONTE: Of course you would! And friends, with *all* good things to eat, it takes a cup of rich, satisfying coffee to "top it off." And that coffee has to be just as fragrantly tempting, just as delicious, just as satisfying as the foods that go with it.

And if you take a tip from me ... in your home *that* coffee will be Maxwell House. The superb blend created by Joel Cheek more than fifty years ago for the patrons of Nashville's famous old hotel.

Millions of Americans have discovered the extra enjoyment that Maxwell House can bring them. In fact, Maxwell House Coffee is sold in more stores than any other coffee in America. And *more* people are enjoying Maxwell House this year than ever before in its history. Yes ... Maxwell House Coffee has won the favor of the world's greatest nation of coffee lovers!

ANNOUNCER: And no wonder ... because Joel Cheek's original Maxwell House Blend is even richer, more delicious, more downright satisfying than ever before. This new perfection of flavor ... full-bodied and mellow ... comes from an extra measure of extra flavor coffees ... highland grown coffees from remote and fertile plantations of Central and South America.

So, friends, when you serve good things to eat, make sure the coffee you serve with them is just as full flavored ... just as delicious.

Discover for yourself the deep down satisfaction in

	Maxwell House Coffee … the coffee that's now … more than ever … good to the last drop.
	(PLAY OFF)
CONTE:	That was lovely, Meredith.
STAFFORD:	John, has Frank left yet?
CONTE:	I think so, Daddy. Say, tell me something, will you? Did Frank win twelve dollars from you the other night?
STAFFORD:	Why, no. We were supposed to have a friendly little card game but I had to call it off.
CONTE:	I thought so. Why didn't you play?
STAFFORD:	Snooks, again. I don't know what I'm going to do with that child. Even on Father's Day she had to misbehave. After I gave her a dollar, too.
CONTE:	What happened?
STAFFORD:	Well, as you know, Frank was supposed to come over, so I sent Snooks out for a deck of cards. I gave her another dollar and she disappeared for over two hours. I got worried, and called up the drugstore, and— (FADES)
	(SNOOKS PLAY-ON)
FATHER:	Hello … Mr. Limp? This is Mr. Higgins. Has Snooks been in your store … oh. Oh, I see … two dollars … Mmm-hmm … Didn't even ask for cards, eh? … Well, thank you, Mr. Limp — goodbye. (HANGS UP)
SOUND:	(DOOR OPENS AND CLOSES)
FATHER:	Snooks! Snooks! Is that you?
BRICE:	Meow! Meow!
FATHER:	Snooks! Is that you, Snooks?
BRICE:	It's only the cat, Daddy. Meow!

FATHER:	Cat, eh? Come into this room at once!
BRICE:	Hello, Daddy.
FATHER:	Where were you tip-toeing so stealthily, my child?
BRICE:	Huh?
FATHER:	Why did you try to sneak upstairs?
BRICE:	Mummy told me to clean Robespierre's room. He's gonna help me.
FATHER:	How nice!
BRICE:	Yeah. Yesterday I made the bed with him … and today I'm gonna mop up the floor with him.
FATHER:	What a helpful little girl you turned out to be.
BRICE:	Yeah. I think I'll—
FATHER:	Just a minute! Before you engage in your domestic duties, I think you should come into this room and close the door behind you.
BRICE:	Why?
FATHER:	Because we're going to have a little pow-wow.
BRICE:	Huh?
FATHER:	I said we're going to have a little pow-wow!
BRICE:	Did the dog have pups?
FATHER:	The dog did not have pups!
BRICE:	Why?
FATHER:	In the first place our dog is a male, and secondly, it's entirely irrelevant!
BRICE:	I thought it was an Airedale.
FATHER:	It is an Airedale!
BRICE:	Well, can't Airedales have—

FATHER:	Airedales can have anything any other dog can have!
BRICE:	Can they have Scotties?
FATHER:	Snooks, I didn't call you in here to discuss dog breeding! And I don't want to talk about dogs at all!
BRICE:	You wanna talk about cats?
FATHER:	No!
BRICE:	Why?
FATHER:	Because I don't! I called you in this room because I have a bone to pick with you.
BRICE:	We're back to the dogs again, Daddy.
FATHER:	Don't be facetious! Sit down!
BRICE:	Yes, Daddy.
FATHER:	Now! Look at the clock!
BRICE:	I'm looking, Daddy.
FATHER:	What time is it?
BRICE:	It's Maxwell House Coff—
FATHER:	We've done that!
BRICE:	I wanna do it again!
FATHER:	Snooks!
BRICE:	I wanna do it again!
FATHER:	Stop it! You should have been here two hours ago!
BRICE:	Why, what happened?
FATHER:	Nothing happened! Snooks, didn't I send you on an errand earlier this evening? Or could it be that my imagination is playing tricks? Could that be?
BRICE:	Could be?

FATHER:	Be very careful, Snooks. I'm in no mood to tolerate any nonsense tonight. Two hours ago I gave you two dollars. Is that right?
BRICE:	Uh-huh.
FATHER:	I told you you might keep one of those dollars for yourself. Is that right?
BRICE:	Uh-huh.
FATHER:	With the other dollar I asked you to purchase a packet of playing cards, so I could play poker. Is that right?
BRICE:	Mummy says it ain't but you keep on playing just the —
FATHER:	Never mind what Mummy says! I'll live my life without being regimented by Mummy!
BRICE:	Ooooh, Daddy.
FATHER:	Wipe that smirk off your face! Now, what happened after you left the house?
BRICE:	I lost one of the dollars.
FATHER:	Well, where are my cards?
BRICE:	I didn't get no cards.
FATHER:	Why not?
BRICE:	'Cause it was your dollar I lost.
FATHER:	Oh, I see. My dollar. Then you still have one dollar left, I take it.
BRICE:	You can't take it 'cause I ain't got it.
FATHER:	Where is it?
BRICE:	Where is what?
FATHER:	The second dollar!
BRICE:	You didn't ask me how I lost the first dollar yet.

FATHER: All right—how did you lose the first dollar?

BRICE: I dunno.

FATHER: That's wonderful! I try to be a good father to you—give you everything you want—and you consistently take advantage of me!

BRICE: I didn't do nothing.

FATHER: And to think you pulled such a trick on this day of all days!

BRICE: It's the only day you gave me a dollar.

FATHER: I'm not talking about that! Do you know what day this is?

BRICE: Dollar Day?

FATHER: No—it's Father's Day! Why do you think I gave you that extra dollar?

BRICE: Because you didn't want me to tell Mummy you were gonna play poker with—

FATHER: Nothing of the kind! I thought you might be decent enough to buy your poor old Daddy a little present! Instead of that you squander the money and come back with a flock of untruths.

BRICE: No, Daddy.

FATHER: Well, tell me the truth then! What did you do with the two dollars?

BRICE: I bought you a present.

FATHER: Oh. What kind of present?

BRICE: A bicycle.

FATHER: You bought me a bicycle? For two dollars?

BRICE: It didn't have no wheels.

FATHER: I see. Well, where is it?

BRICE:	I was riding it home and—
FATHER:	Wait a minute! How could you ride the bicycle if it had no wheels?
BRICE:	It had pedals.
FATHER:	What good are pedals without wheels?
BRICE:	That's what I said. So I threw the whole thing away.
FATHER:	All right, Snooks, I'm not going to bandy words with you any longer. I want the truth right now! What did you do with the money?
BRICE:	(CRYING) I lost it in a poker game!
FATHER:	I told you I want the truth! Tell me everything that happened from the moment you left this house! You had the two dollars, didn't you?
BRICE:	Uh-huh.
FATHER:	Well?
BRICE:	Well, I started to go to the drugstore—and they grabbed the money!
FATHER:	Who grabbed the money?
BRICE:	The four burglars.
FATHER:	What four burglars?
BRICE:	What did you say, Daddy?
FATHER:	You said four burglars grabbed the money! (OMINOUSLY) Well—I'm waiting!
BRICE:	I'm thinking, Daddy.
FATHER:	Are these the same four burglars that made you play hooky from school, and made you break the window, and made you tear up my stamp collection?
BRICE:	Yeah. What do they want from me, Daddy?

FATHER:	I know what I want from you! I want the truth! This is a very serious matter and I won't accept any cock-and-bull stories!
BRICE:	Why?
FATHER:	Because that burglar stuff has worn thin — you don't think I'm going to fall for that yarn about four burglars anymore, do you?
BRICE:	How about five burglars?
FATHER:	Oh, come, Snooks — you can do better than that.
BRICE:	I know I can, but you're rushing me.
FATHER:	Listen to me, Snooks, it'll be so much easier for you if you just tell the truth. Then you won't have to bother making up those fantastic stories.
BRICE:	It ain't no bother, Daddy.
FATHER:	Well, this is the last time I'll let you listen to Frank Morgan! Now come on—tell me what happened to the money. The truth this time!
BRICE:	All right, Daddy. I'll tell you the truth.
FATHER:	That's better! The absolute truth!
BRICE:	Yes, Daddy.
FATHER:	Go on. What happened to the money?
BRICE:	I was holding it in my hand like this—
FATHER:	Yes?
BRICE:	And when I pushed out my hand it got stuck on his horn.
FATHER:	Whose horn?
BRICE:	The tiger's horn. He started to—
FATHER:	Stop it! Are you trying to tell me you saw a tiger?

BRICE:	Uh-huh.
FATHER:	With a horn?
BRICE:	He was driving a car. Then a lion jumped on the running board and—
FATHER:	Ohhh! Lions and tigers! I'm going to see this thing through to the bitter end.
BRICE:	That's what the lion did to the tiger, Daddy.
FATHER:	What?
BRICE:	He bit her en—
FATHER:	Snooks! I've had enough of this!
BRICE:	Me, too—goodnight, Daddy!
FATHER:	Stay here! I just called Mr. Limp at the drugstore and he told me you spent the two dollars on candy and ice cream!
BRICE:	Did he?
FATHER:	He did! Now, I suppose you're ready to drop your hocus-pocus?
BRICE:	I'll take 'em off if you want me to, Daddy.
FATHER:	I mean are you ready to confess?
BRICE:	Yes, Daddy. I spent the money.
FATHER:	Well, that's that. But I can't see for the life of me how you managed to do away with two dollars worth of candy and ice cream all by yourself!
BRICE:	I didn't eat it, Daddy.
FATHER:	Then who did?
BRICE:	Nobody. I hid it in the closet. I wanted to make a party for you.
FATHER:	You wanted—Snooks.

BRICE:	Here it is, Daddy. Look at it.
FATHER:	Ohh! Ohh—I feel terrible. Why didn't you tell me?
BRICE:	I wanted to surprise you. Shall I turn over?
FATHER:	No, I have got a better idea. I'll turn over!
BRICE:	Why?
FATHER:	You can spank me! I deserve it.
BRICE:	I got the best idea, Daddy.
FATHER:	What is it?
BRICE:	Let's both spank Robespierre! (LAUGHS)
FATHER:	Oh, nonsense! Come on—let's have the party!
BRICE:	Happy Father's Day, Daddy!
FATHER:	My baby!
	(MUSIC ... APPLAUSE)
	COMMERCIAL
CLOSING—140 WORDS-48 SECONDS
ANNOUNCER:	Friends, to help you enjoy a full measure of flavor and goodness with Maxwell House Coffee, we offer you three Maxwell House grinds—one of them correct for your way of making coffee!

For you who use glass coffee makers, there's the *new* glass-maker grind Maxwell House ... prepared in answer to your demands ... and especially *pulverized* for glass coffee makers. It gives you clear, sparkling coffee with all the full, rich flavor of the *new* Maxwell House. It's *brand* new. But if your grocer doesn't have it, he can quickly order it.

Of course, Maxwell House comes also in *regular grind* for percolator or coffee pot ... and drip grind for drip methods of making coffee.

So tomorrow, why not ask for Maxwell House in the |

	grind that's *correct* for *your* way of making coffee? You'll find it perfect coffee ... perfectly ground!
	(MUSIC PLAY-OFF)
	(THEME FADES FOR:)
CONTE:	And that's about all we have time for tonight, ladies and gentlemen, but we'll all be back again next Thursday evening at Maxwell House Coffee Time. Fanny Brice as Baby Snooks, Frank Morgan, who appears with us through the courtesy of Metro-Goldwyn-Mayer, Hanley Stafford, and Meredith Willson.
	Until Next Thursday then, this is John Conte, saying goodnight and good luck from the makers of Maxwell House ... the coffee that's always ... good to the last drop!
	(MUSIC ... APPLAUSE)

MAXWELL HOUSE
Presents
"GOOD NEWS OF 1940"
JULY 18, 1940

1. REUBEN AND RACHEL - MARTIN - POWELL
2. "I CAN'T LOVE YOU ANY MORE" —DICK POWELL
3. COMMERCIAL
4. BABY SNOOKS —BRICE-STAFFORD
5. "SPANISH DANCE" —ORCHESTRA
6. COMMERCIAL
7. STRAUSS MEDLEY —MARY MARTIN
8. SNOOKS' COMPOSITION, "THE GOAT" —FANNY BRICE
9. "I'M A TOUGH HOMBRE" —DICK POWELL
10. SIGN-OFF

HULL: Maxwell House Coffee presents — Good News of 1940!

("ALWAYS AND ALWAYS" FADES FOR)

POWELL: Good evening. This is Dick Powell inviting you to another Good News get-together with Fanny Brice as Baby Snooks — Hanley Stafford as Daddy — lovely Mary Martin — Warren Hull and Meredith Willson and his music.

And, folks, right now's the time to join us in our famous Maxwell House custom. So pull up your chairs and relax over a fragrant, full-bodied cup of the coffee that's … good to the last drop!

Well, we've had the roll call, ladies and gentlemen,

and all the members appear to be present and in good standing, so let's call this here meeting to order. According to the list that Brother Willson handed me, I see that we're due for a bit of a duet called Reuben and Rachel. Now, that sounds like real nice, down to home stuff so let's all get together and see if we can't make it hum. Step out here, Sister Martin.

(APPLAUSE)

MARTIN: Thank you.

POWELL: You look right purty tonight, Sister.

MARTIN: You don't look like uphill hay yourself, Brother.

POWELL: Thank you. Makes me feel young again to hear you talk like that. How's chances of washing up this here Reuben and Rachel jive?

MARTIN: Shoot the towel to me, Powell.

POWELL: Well, it's a clean start anyway. Maestro!

MERE: Yes, by cracky?

POWELL: Will you start sending?

MERE: By cracky, yes!

POWELL: That's a switch. Hit it, Farmer Willson, and let's plow!

REUBEN - RACHEL - POWELL - MARTIN

(APPLAUSE)

POWELL: Thank you, Mary — thank you, ladies and gentlemen. Oh yes, and thank you, too, Meredith, for that delightful, bucolic arrangement.

MERE: Think nothing of it, Dickie boy. It gives me pleasure to play anything with a farm flavor. Something wholesome about it.

POWELL: Yes. Well, as —

MERE:	You'd never know it to look at me, but I used to be a farm lad, myself, Dick.
POWELL:	Well, I must say your disguise is perfect. But I think —
MERE:	You know, I was raised in a swell little town, Mason City, Iowa — and my folks had a small farm. We had the south forty in corn.
POWELL:	In corn, eh? Well, that's very —
MERE:	Every year when harvest time came around, it was my job to bring in the corn.
POWELL:	Times certainly change, don't they?
MERE:	They sure do.
POWELL:	Now you dish it out.
MERE:	Yes. Huh?
POWELL:	Nothing. I was just wondering, Meredith, have you ever gone back to visit the town of your nativity?
MERE:	Who?
POWELL:	Do you ever go back to Mason City?
MERE:	Do I. Go every year like clockwork! When I get my vacation, the first thing I do is say, "Peggy" —
BOTH:	That's Mrs. Willson.
MERE:	Yes. By gum, Dick — why do I keep telling you who Peggy is? I believe you know her as well as I do!
POWELL:	Come, come, Meredith — after all, I've only met her about thirty or forty times.
MERE:	You have? Well, I guess it's just a nasty habit.
POWELL:	Meeting Peggy?
MERE:	No — I mean explaining who she is.

POWELL: That's all right, old man. It's a common failing — explaining one's wife.

MERE: I guess so. Well, anyway — when I get my vacation, the first thing I do is say, "Peggy! Let's hop right on the train and go to Mason City."

POWELL: And what does she say?

MERE: Er — she says no. But don't misunderstand, Dick — she just wants to save it for the last part of the vacation — sort of like dessert.

POWELL: I see. Mason City a la mode, as it were.

MERE: As it were. (SHEEPISH LAUGH)

POWELL: Yes. (SAME THING)

MERE: Yes. Well, the first part of our vacation is usually rather a hit and run affair — can't make up our minds between Honolulu — Banff — Grand Canyon — all that stuff. Just like last year.

POWELL: Where did you go last year?

MERE: We stayed home.

POWELL: Well, that's a nice spot — little too commercial, though. Don't you think?

MERE: The food is good.

POWELL: Yes. Well, what places are you going to argue about visiting this year, Meredith?

MERE: No arguments this year. I'm not taking any vacation.

POWELL: No vacation! Why not? Every man needs a little rest in the summer.

MERE: Fiddle-faddle! June, July, August — and the summer is gone! Besides, I've taken on a little extra work. You know about the Chaplin picture

POWELL:	I know you're arranging the score for it. But that won't take you all summer.
MERE:	No — but what about the Johnson Wax Program?
POWELL:	What about it?
MERE:	Well, I — or — I have a little revue that goes on Thursday nights for Johnson's Wax.
POWELL:	That's two plugs in two lines. And some people think you're naïve. Well, just answer my first question. Are you going back to Mason City this year?
MERE:	Probably. But I don't call that a vacation.
POWELL:	I see what you mean.
MERE:	Now, don't get me wrong, Dick —
POWELL:	Of course not. Mason City will understand. But in the meantime, it's a little too early for me to start my vacation so how about backing me up with two choruses of "I Can't Love You Any More"?
MERE:	I'm right behind you, Dickie.
POWELL:	Then start pushing, lovey. Gotta jump off somewhere!
	"I CAN'T LOVE YOU ANY MORE" —POWELL & ORCHESTRA
POWELL:	Friends, today more people are enjoying Maxwell House Coffee than ever before in its history! More stores sell Maxwell House than any other coffee in America! Naturally, there's a reason for this extraordinary preference ...
HULL:	(IN FAST) ... and friends, it's just this! Today, there's extra coffee pleasure in Maxwell House, the likes of which you've never known! And yet this famous coffee is selling today at the lowest prices in history!
	You see ... ever since Maxwell House was first introduced more than fifty years ago, we've worked

unceasingly to bring you the finest possible coffee at the lowest possible price!

Year after year, as better coffees become available, we've searched them out … blended them with a knowledge and skill born of half a century's invaluable experience in the coffee business. We've developed the unique, "radiant roast" process to roast this superb blend to perfection … the famous blue super-vacuum tin to bring it to you roaster-fresh!

And now today … into every pound of Maxwell House … go highland-grown, premium coffees from the plateaus of far-off Central and South America … extra-flavored coffees now available in quantities sufficient to supply the great Maxwell House demand! Each adds its separate, superb quality of flavor, body, or fragrance to further enrich the famous Maxwell House blend.

And yet, Maxwell House is selling today at the lowest prices ever … prices you may have paid for ordinary coffee just a few short months ago! Per cup, Maxwell House now costs but a fraction of a cent more than cheapest coffees sold!

Have you tried Maxwell House lately? If not, this weekend's none too soon to discover the extra goodness in this famous coffee that's now, more than ever … good to the last drop!

(CHORD — FADES FOR)

POWELL: And now, ladies and gentlemen, here is Fanny Brice as Baby Snooks!

(MUSIC … APPLAUSE)

POWELL: Well, Daddy, played by Hanley Stafford, is putting on a minstrel show for his lodge. In order to make a thorough job of it, Daddy has decided to visit the public library for technical research and to browse through a few joke books. Naturally, he shouldn't escape the clutches of his dynamic offspring so we find them both on the steps of the library. Listen …

FATHER:	Now, Snooks, before we go in you must understand one thing.
BRICE:	No noise.
FATHER:	Exactly. You must be as quiet as a mouse — don't raise your voice above a whisper and walk on your tip-toes.
BRICE:	Is anybody dead in there?
FATHER:	Nobody's dead in there! But a lot of people come to the library to cogitate.
BRICE:	Don't they feel good, Daddy?
FATHER:	They feel fine. But people who go to the library don't wish to be disturbed while they're meditating. That's why you'll behave better than you ever have before!
BRICE:	Will I?
FATHER:	You will if you want to go in with me.
BRICE:	I will.
FATHER:	All right. Then let's go — but remember — conduct yourself like a little lady. Comprehend?
BRICE:	Copperhead.
FATHER:	Very well.
BRICE:	Wait a minute, Daddy.
FATHER:	What is it?
BRICE:	I got a noisy feeling coming over me.
FATHER:	Snooks! I warned you!
BRICE:	It's gone now, Daddy. I'll be very quiet.
FATHER:	Okay. Hold on to my hand.
BRICE:	What's in the library, Daddy?
FATHER:	Books. Thousands of books.

BRICE: Did Uncle Louie make them?

FATHER: No, of course not.

BRICE: Well, mummy said that Uncle Louie was a bookmaker when —

FATHER: Never mind that! Just don't snoop around so much! And don't repeat everything you hear!

BRICE: Why?

FATHER: Because that's gossiping! Leave that to your mother!

BRICE: Huh?

FATHER: Nothing! Trouble with all women — if there were just three women left in the world do you know what they'd do?

BRICE: No.

FATHER: Two of them would get together and talk about the other one!

BRICE: Why?

FATHER: Because they would!

BRICE: If there was three men left in the world what would they do?

FATHER: I don't know. Come on in.

BRICE: Would they get together and look for the three women?

FATHER: Forget about the men and women. We're going inside now, so be quiet.

BRICE: Who's that man behind the desk?

FATHER: Shhh. He's the librarian. I have to talk to him. Er — excuse me.

RUBIN: (VERY QUIET, MEEK MAN) Yes sir. May I help you, sir?

BRICE: What's he scared about, Daddy?

FATHER: Shhh. I told you not to raise your voice. Keep quiet.

BRICE: I wanna picture book.

FATHER: Just a minute. Er — I'm looking for some books on minstrelsy.

RUBIN: Certainly. Have you any particular book in mind?

FATHER: No. I'm putting on a —

BRICE: I wanna picture book!

RUBIN: Careful, sweetheart! Mustn't climb up on my desk. (PATIENT LAUGH)

FATHER: Snooks, come off of that desk. I'm awfully sorry.

RUBIN: Oh, she didn't hurt anything. Lively little thing, isn't she?

FATHER: (HISSES) Snooks, what did I tell you before we came in?

BRICE: Well, I wanna picture book.

RUBIN: There are lots of picture books on the shelves over there. I'll see what I can find for you in the meantime, sir.

FATHER: Come on, Snooks.

BRICE: Where are we going?

FATHER: Into the reading room.

SOUND: (DOOR OPEN AND CLOSES)

BRICE: Daddy!

FATHER: Shhh! Snooks — don't you see that sign on the wall?

BRICE: What sign?

FATHER: (Whispers) Right there! (SPELLS) S-I-L-E-N-C-E.

BRICE:	Well, I ain't smoking.
FATHER:	(WHISPERS) It says silence!
BRICE:	Huh?
FATHER:	(LOUD) Silence!
NELSON:	Please! Is there no place a soul can commune with the masters?
FATHER:	I'm sorry, sir. She'll be quiet.
NELSON:	Thank you. Hmmm.
BRICE:	Is this the reading room, Daddy?
FATHER:	Yes.
BRICE:	Well, why is that man writing?
FATHER:	Because he wants to write.
BRICE:	Well, why don't he go to the writing room?
FATHER:	There isn't any writing room.
BRICE:	Well, you said this is the reading room.
FATHER:	It is. But people stand in sitting rooms, don't they?
BRICE:	Why?
FATHER:	I don't know. Maybe it's because there's only standing room.
BRICE:	Is it a standing room or a sitting room?
FATHER:	It's a sitting room.
BRICE:	Then why don't they sit down?
FATHER:	Because there's no sitting room!
BRICE:	Well, how can —
FATHER:	Oh, keep quiet! You're irritating that man, Snooks.
BRICE:	Well, I wanna picture book!

FATHER:	I'll find you one in a minute.
NELSON:	Oh, this is really too much!
FATHER:	Excuse me, sir. Come over here, Snooks.
BRICE:	That man's got a picture book, Daddy.
FATHER:	It's not the kind you want.
BRICE:	Why?
FATHER:	Because it's a book on archeology.
BRICE:	What's that?
FATHER:	It's the study of lost races.
BRICE:	Did you write it?
FATHER:	No!
BRICE:	Well, you never win.
FATHER:	It has nothing to do with horse races — and you mind your own business.
NELSON:	Please!
FATHER:	Excuse me. See — you'll cause me plenty of trouble before I get out of here. Here's a picture book — sit down and look at it.
BRICE:	I want that book up there.
FATHER:	No. That's a book about reincarnation.
BRICE:	I like flowers.
FATHER:	Reincarnation isn't about flowers. It's a theory that when you leave this world, you return again in some other form.
BRICE:	Could I come back as a devil?
FATHER:	No — you can't be the same thing twice. Here — look at these wonderful pictures. They're all famous paintings.

BRICE:	What's this one, daddy?
FATHER:	It's called "Faith." See the boat being tossed about by the high waves?
BRICE:	Uh-huh.
FATHER:	And notice the sailor with his hands raised to Heaven. He has faith that he'll be rescued.
BRICE:	What's faith, daddy?
FATHER:	Well, you can see the boat and you can see the sailor — but if I told you there was a frankfurter on that boat and you believed me — that would be faith. Understand?
BRICE:	Understand.
FATHER:	Well, what is faith?
BRICE:	A frankfurter on a boat.
FATHER:	That's right.
BRICE:	I'm smart, ain't I, daddy?
FATHER:	Brilliant. Look at the pictures.
BRICE:	I wanna look at that man's book.
FATHER:	Snooks — come back here.
BRICE:	Hello, mister.
NELSON:	I prefer to be left alone.
BRICE:	Why?
NELSON:	Excuse me, sir, is this your daughter?
FATHER:	Yes.
NELSON:	What do you call this sweet little child?
FATHER:	Snooks.
NELSON:	Then for heavens sakes — call her!

BRICE:	I wanna see his pictures.
FATHER:	Snooks — you heard what the man said! Come away from there at once!
BRICE:	I wanna see what he's writing.
NELSON:	Take your hands off my precious notes! Stop her!
FATHER:	Snooks!
BRICE:	I only wanna — (TEARING PAPER)
NELSON:	Ohhh! She's torn them!
FATHER:	That's the last straw!
BRICE:	Let's go home, Daddy.
RUBIN:	Oh, there you are. Here are your minstrel books, sir.
NELSON:	Minstrel books! For forty years, I've worked on this masterpiece only to have it wrecked by a blackface comedian and his pickaninny!
FATHER:	I'm sure you can piece those papers together again — I know —
NELSON:	Out of my sight! Take them away!
RUBIN:	You'd better leave, sir. He gets very violent.
FATHER:	All right. Come with me, Snooks.
BRICE:	Where are we going, Daddy?
FATHER:	Shhh. This is a library and you must be very quiet.
BRICE:	Awight.
FATHER:	Let me close that door.
SOUND:	(DOOR CLOSES)
BRICE:	Can't you wait till we get home, Daddy?
FATHER:	I'm sorry, Snooks — but this must be attended to right now!

BRICE: Oh. Shall I turn over.

FATHER: Place yourself across that bench. Thank you.

BRICE: You're welcome, Daddy.

FATHER: Ready?

BRICE: Ready.

FATHER: Well — here we go again. (HE SPANKS HER FOUR TIMES)

BRICE: Finished?

FATHER: Yes. And Snooks, although you thoroughly deserved it — it hurt me worse than it did you.

BRICE: I knew it would, Daddy.

FATHER: What do you mean?

BRICE: 'Cause I stuck that picture book in my panties! (LAUGHS)

FATHER: You little — (SOCK)

BRICE: WAAAAHHHHH!

(MUSIC ... APPLAUSE)

POWELL: Thank you, Baby Snooks, and Daddy, and company. They'll return in a jiffy, folks, but right now, let's all settle back and enjoy Meredith Willson's old Parlor Piece for this evening. He opens his Maxwell House Album and presents a musical picture of Moskowski's unforgettable composition — Spanish Dance. Grab your castanets and start clicking, maestro.

"SPANISH DANCE" —ORCHESTRA

(APPLAUSE)

HULL: Friends ... if you haven't tried Maxwell House lately ... let me tell you what you can look forward to.

First of all ... the matchless flavor and goodness for

which Maxwell House has been famous more than fifty years. And today, with extra-flavored, highland-grown coffees blended into every pound, the celebrated Maxwell House blend is richer, more fragrantly full-bodied, than ever before!

Then, too, you'll enjoy coffee at the peak of its fresh flavor and fragrance because Maxwell House comes to you sealed in the famous blue super-vacuum can . . . not just day's fresh, but roaster fresh!

And best of all . . . you'll discover that with all its extra flavor and goodness . . . Maxwell House is selling right now at the lowest prices in history!

Order a pound tomorrow! For now … more than ever … is the time to … make friends with Maxwell House!

(MUSIC BRIDGE)

POWELL: Thank you, Warren. And you'll all do well to heed the sage advice of Warren the Hull, ladies, and gentlemen. Now, here's the green light, which means it's time for me to produce once again our delightful Maxwell House songstress. Here she is, the lady whose beauty beggars description, as they say in the pulp magazines, the wonderful, winsome wench from Weatherford, Mary Martin. For her solo tonight, Mary offers a specially arranged medley of waltzes from the brilliant pen of Johann Strauss. It's all yours, Mary.

STRAUSS MEDLEY —MARTIN & ORCHESTRA

(APPLAUSE)

POWELL: That was beautiful, Mary. And now, here is Baby Snooks with a brand new animal composition. Bring her on, Daddy.

STAFF: Okay, Dick. All right, Snooks.

BRICE: Can I read it now?

STAFF: Right now.

BRICE: Awight, Daddy … Composition on the camel. The camel is the funniest animal in the world. He's got feet like a duck, a face like a moose, a body like a roller coaster, and knock-knees like my Aunt Sophie.

STAFF: Snooks! I want you to confine yourself to the camel and eliminate all other remarks. Aunt Sophie is not knock-kneed.

BRICE: How do you know, Daddy?

STAFF: Oh, go on!

BRICE: The camel looks awful — but he is a noble animal. He also has a noble smell. I don't see how he can stand himself. Camels live in the desert and they are very smart. They make coats, brushes, and cigarettes.

STAFF: They do nothing of the kind!

BRICE: Why?

STAFF: I'll explain later. Keep on reading.

BRICE: Some camels have two humps and some camels have one hump. The ones with two humps look like a cow upside down. You can ride on their backs but you must sit between the two humps, otherwise, it will tickle you. I hope you get the point. Camels are the only animal in the world that can live for thirty days without water. I don't believe it.

STAFF: Well, it happens to be true!

BRICE: But you said Uncle Louie didn't touch water for thirty years.

STAFF: Never mind that! Finish your composition. And tell that joke.

BRICE: Awight. My daddy told me a little joke about camels. He said they never get hungry on the desert because they can always eat the sand-which-is there. I think that joke smells as bad as the camel. The end.

	(APPLAUSE)
DICK:	Oh, Mary!
MARY:	Yes, Dick?
DICK:	Oh, you ain't seen nothin' yet, my little Texas pet, til you get a load of me out on the range.
MARY:	Ah'll believe it when I see it.
DICK:	Are you belittlin'?
MARY:	Far be it. But the thought of you in buckskin seems quite strange.
DICK:	Oh, is that so? Well, I'm a tough hombre!
	(INSERT FOR SONG)
POWELL:	Howdy, ma'am. I've been riding all day to get to you, gal.
MARTIN:	Hi, cowboy. Shake the dust from your chaps and tie up your bronc.
POWELL:	Ma'am. I ain't aimin' to beat around no bush today — I come to ask you to marry me.
MARTIN:	I can't, pardner. I swore the cuss I marry will be the best shot in Sneak Gulch — and when I swear, cowboy, I mean it!
POWELL:	There ain't no better shot in Sneak Gulch than me, gal. I'll prove it.
MARTIN:	Careful with that hoss-pistol.
POWELL:	Watch me blast that acorn off'n that oak.
SOUND:	(PISTOL SHOT)
POWELL:	How's that?
BRICE:	No good. Ah kin shoot better'n that with my eyes closed.

POWELL: Waaal — who's the little varmint, ma'am?

MARTIN: She's my kid sis. Raised in the saddle, fed on cactus, and cut her teeth on a forty-five.

BRICE: Yippee! Where's my bronc — I feel like bull-doggin' a few steers!

POWELL: Let's see kin you shoot that owl, sis?

BRICE: Hand me yer shootin' iron, pardner.

MARTIN: Remember, cowboy — if she beats you shootin' I ain't agoin' ter marry you.

POWELL: It's a deal. Start blastin', sis.

BRICE: What'll I shoot at, cowboy?

POWELL: See that humming bird on the top branch of that tree about two hundred yards away?

BRICE: Ah sees it.

POWELL: Waaal — shoot him in the eye.

BRICE: Okay. Which eye, pardner?

POWELL: If you can shoot him in any eye — I'll give up yore sister.

BRICE: Ah'll shoot from the hip. (PISTOL SHOT) Guess that done it, sis.

POWELL: Shucks. Waaal — I guess it's back to the fillin' station fer me.

MARTIN: So long, cowboy.

BRICE: Come around tomorrow and ah'll show you some fancy ropin'. Yippee!

(INTO SONG)

("ALWAYS AND ALWAYS" ... FADES FOR)

HULL: For another big half-hour of fun, stay tuned to this

network for the "Aldrich Family," which follows immediately over most of these same stations.

And next week at this same time, and *every* week, tune in Good News and the "Aldrich Family" for a solid hour of grand Thursday evening entertainment!

Until next Thursday then, this is Warren Hull bidding you goodnight and good luck for the makers of Maxwell House — the coffee that's always — good to the last drop!

(MUSIC ... FULL AND OUT ON CUE)

GIBNEY: Now ... important news ... about your favorite corn flakes! Post Toasties are now enriched with vitamin B-1 ... the energy vitamin authorities say we all need every day!

Lack of vitamin B-1 may cause fatigue, poor appetite, and nervousness. Growing children *especially* need vitamin B-1! Now Post Toasties and *no other corn flakes* give you this *extra* value at *no extra cost!*

So tomorrow, start serving *your* family crisp, delicious Post Toasties *every day.*

This is the National Broadcasting Company.

MAXWELL HOUSE
Presents
"GOOD NEWS OF 1940"
JULY 25, 1940

1. "I CRIED FOR YOU" —MARTIN-POWELL
2. "SPANISH DANCE" —ORCHESTRA
3. COMMERCIAL
4. BABY SNOOKS —FANNY BRICE AND HANLEY STAFFORD
5. "FOOLS RUSH IN" —DICK POWELL
6. COMMERCIAL
7. "THE BREEZE AND I" —MARY MARTIN
8. SNOOKS' COMPOSITION —FANNY BRICE
10. SIGN-OFF —MARTIN - POWELL - CHOIR

HULL: Maxwell House Coffee presents — Good News of 1940!

("ALWAYS AND ALWAYS" FADES FOR)

POWELL: Good evening. This is Dick Powell inviting you to another Good News get-together with Fanny Brice as Baby Snooks — Hanley Stafford as Daddy — lovely Mary Martin — Warren Hull and Meredith Willson and his music.

And right now ... it's coffee time. Time to join with us in the enjoyment of a rich, full-bodied cup of Maxwell House ... coffee that's now ... more than ever ... good to the last drop.

Well, dear friends, I might as well break the news to you now — tonight the Maxwell House Show will call a halt to festivities for the next five weeks. During those vacation days, some of us will pursue the elusive trout, some of us will take to the open road in our panting jalopies, and some of us will just stay home in our jalopping panties. Personally, I'm a catboat man and I really mean to do some heavy meowing.

However, there's still work to be done and it wouldn't be right if we didn't leave you in a blaze of glory — so I'll call on the most glorious blaze I can think of — steaming, fragrant Mary Martin!

(APPLAUSE)

MARTIN: Thank you. You might add, Dickie boy, that I'm now, more than ever, good to the last drop!

POWELL: That goes without saying, sugar-puss. Now how about ripping off a little duet?

MARTIN: Let 'er rip!

POWELL: Maestro — a snazzy introduction and two choruses of "I Cried for You" — if you please!

"I CRIED FOR YOU" —POWELL & MARTIN

POWELL: Thank you, ladies and gentlemen — and thank you, Mary.

BRICE: Hello.

POWELL: Well, hello, Snooks. What brings you here so early?

BRICE: I wanna ask you something, Mr. Powell.

POWELL: Shoot.

BRICE: Can I go with you on your vacation?

POWELL: Well — er — isn't your daddy taking you somewhere this year?

BRICE: No. He's a very nasty daddy and he's gonna keep me chained up in the cellar and —

STAFF: Snooks! What did you just say?

BRICE:	I didn't say nothing, daddy.
STAFF:	I heard what you said — and if you dare say such things again —
POWELL:	Hold it, daddy. What's happened?
STAFF:	Plenty. I'll tell you about it later, Dick. In the meantime, you come with me, young lady.
BRICE:	Why?
STAFF:	I want to have a talk with you.
BRICE:	Yeah — but you ain't gonna talk.
STAFF:	We'll see about that! Come on!
BRICE:	Awight. I'll see you later, Mr. Powell.
POWELL:	Okay, Snooks.
MERE:	What do you suppose she's been up to now, Dick?
POWELL:	I can't imagine — but we'll hear the story from daddy, no doubt. Well, Meredith — I suppose you have your vacation all planned.
MERE:	Yes sir. Plenty planned. Yes sir!
POWELL:	Yes sir. Meredith, I was just wondering — have you ever gone back to visit the town of your nativity?
MERE:	Who?
POWELL:	Do you ever go back to Mason City?
MERE:	Do I? Go every year like clockwork. When I get my vacation the first thing I do is say, "Peggy —"
BOTH:	That's Mrs. Willson.
MERE:	Yes. By gum, Dick — why do I keep telling you who Peggy is? I believe you know her as well as I do!
POWELL:	Come, come Meredith — after all, I've only met her about thirty or forty times.

MERE: You have? Well, I guess it's just a nasty habit.

POWELL: Meeting Peggy?

MERE: No — I mean explaining who she is.

POWELL: That's all right, old man. It's a common failing — explaining one's wife.

MERE: I guess so. Well, anyway — when I get my vacation, the first thing I do is say, "Peggy! Let's hop right on the train and go to Mason City."

POWELL: And what does she say?

MERE: Er — she says no. But don't misunderstand, Dick — she just wants to save it for the last part of the vacation — sort of like a dessert.

POWELL: I see. Mason City a la mode, as it were.

MERE: As it were. (SHEEPISH LAUGH)

POWELL: Yes. (SAME THING)

MERE: Yes. Well, the first part of our vacation is usually rather a hit and run affair — can't make up our minds between Honolulu — Banff — Grand Canyon — all that stuff. Just like last year.

POWELL: Where did you go last year?

MERE: We stayed home.

POWELL: Well, that's a nice spot — little too commercial, though. Don't you think?

MERE: The food is good.

POWELL: Yes. Well, what places are you going to argue about visiting this year, Meredith?

MERE: No arguments this year. I'm not taking any vacation.

POWELL: No vacation! Why not? Every man needs a little rest in the summer.

MERE: Fiddle-faddle! June, July, August — and the summer is gone! Besides, I've taken on a little extra work. You know about the Chaplin picture —

POWELL: I know you're arranging the score for it. But that won't take you all summer.

MERE: No — but what about the Johnson Wax Program?

POWELL: What about it?

MERE: Well, I — er — I have a little revue that goes on Tuesday nights for Johnson's Wax.

POWELL: That's two plugs in two lines. And some people think you're naïve.

MERE: Yes sir! (LAUGHS)

POWELL: Oh, stop it! And just to stop you from jumping the gun on your vacation — what's the old Parlor Piece for tonight?

MERE: Spanish Dance by Moskowski.

POWELL: Fine. Grab your castanets, Meredith, and start clicking.

SPANISH DANCE ORCHESTRA

(APPLAUSE)

POWELL: When a good thing is made better, that's news enough. But when that better thing costs you less than ever before, it's news that rates a headline. And that's the kind of news Warren Hull has about Maxwell House Coffee tonight.

HULL: Yes, friends ... today, there's extra pleasure in Maxwell House, the likes of which you've never known. And yet, this famous coffee is selling today at the lowest prices in history.

You see, ever since Maxwell House was first introduced more than fifty years ago, we've worked unceasingly to bring you the finest possible coffee at the lowest possible price. Year after year, as better coffees became available, we've searched them out … blended them with a knowledge and skill born of half a century's invaluable experience in the coffee business. We've developed the unique "radian roast" process to roast this superb blend to perfection … the famous blue super-vacuum tin to bring it to you roaster-fresh.

And now today … into every pound of Maxwell House … go highland-grown, premium coffees from the mountain plateaus of far-off Central and South America … extra-flavored coffees now available in quantities sufficient to supply the great Maxwell House demand. Each adds it separate, superb quality of flavor, body, or fragrance to further enrich the famous Maxwell House blend.

And yet, Maxwell House is selling today at the lowest prices ever … prices you may have paid for just ordinary coffee a few short months ago. Per cup, Maxwell House now costs but a fraction of a cent more than cheapest coffees sold. Have you tried Maxwell House lately? If not, discover this very weekend the extra goodness of this coffee that's now … more than ever … good to the last drop.

(CHORD FADES FOR)

POWELL:	Very aptly put, Warren. Now, I'd like to coax daddy out here and see if we can't find out what happened yesterday. Oh, daddy.
STAFF:	Yes, Dick. Well, there isn't much to tell — except that this year, I planned a real vacation. I put away my pennies for a trip to Honolulu.
POWELL:	And you're not going?
STAFF:	I'm afraid not. You see, I had to go down and pick up the tickets and Snooks insisted on coming along. Well — it was a tough battle but, as usual, I yielded.
POWELL:	As usual.

STAFF:	Yes. Well, we drove down to the travel agency, which happened to be right on the waterfront and I had —
	(FADES)
SOUND:	(BOAT WHISTLES)
FATHER:	Come along, Snooks — don't dawdle!
BRICE:	Lookit all the boats, daddy.
FATHER:	We'll look at them later. I have to get my tickets now.
BRICE:	Where we going?
FATHER:	To Honolulu.
BRICE:	Are we going on that big ship, daddy?
FATHER:	No — we're traveling on a passenger ship. That's a freighter.
BRICE:	Afraid of what?
FATHER:	Afraid of nothing! It's a tramp steamer.
BRICE:	A tramp?
FATHER:	Yes! Come on!
SOUND:	(DEEP BOAT WHISTLES)
BRICE:	What's the tramp whistling for, daddy?
FATHER:	Maybe he wants a nickel for a cup of coffee. Hurry up — I must get those tickets or they won't hold them.
BRICE:	I wanna see the boat!
FATHER:	I said you'll see it later.
BRICE:	What are they pulling up in that big net?
FATHER:	That's the freight. It's called the cargo.
BRICE:	Why?
FATHER:	Because it is. Anything that a ship carries is called a

	cargo.
BRICE:	Well, where's the car?
FATHER:	There isn't any car! If it was being carried in a car, it would be called a shipment.
BRICE:	Huh?
FATHER:	That's right. Ships carry cargo and cars carry shipments.
BRICE:	How did they get mixed up?
FATHER:	They're not mixed up! Will you please come with me?
BRICE:	I wanna go on the boat!
FATHER:	Oh — I knew I shouldn't have brought you along! I simply must pick up those tickets right away.
BRICE:	Why?
FATHER:	Because we can't sail without tickets! Do you want to be a stowaway?
BRICE:	Uh-huh.
FATHER:	You would! You listen to me, Snooks — if you don't conduct yourself like a lady all day today, I won't take you on the trip!
BRICE:	Will you leave me home all alone?
FATHER:	Yes!
BRICE:	And will you chain me up in the cellar and let the wolves eat me?
FATHER:	Maybe I will! What do you think of that?
BRICE:	I like it.
FATHER:	That's enough, Snooks — I'm taking you right home!
BRICE:	No, I'll be good, daddy.
FATHER:	Well, all right. Come on in.

SOUND:	(DOOR OPENS AND CLOSES)
RUBIN:	Ah, how do you do, sir?
FATHER:	I have a cabin reserved on the S. S. Malaria.
BRICE:	Is that the name of the boat, daddy?
FATHER:	Yes — shhh. The name is Higgins.
RUBIN:	Higgins.
BRICE:	Lancelot B. Higgins. He's my daddy.
RUBIN:	Well! I'll bet you think he's just about the best daddy in the whole world, don't you?
BRICE:	What'll you bet?
FATHER:	Snooks! Are you commencing?
BRICE:	I'm commencing, daddy.
FATHER:	Well, stop it!
RUBIN:	(LAUGHS) Ah, me! Children, children! Nothing like them, is there, Mr. Higgins?
FATHER:	No, thank Heaven!
RUBIN:	I have five of them myself. (LAUGHS)
FATHER:	Well, what are you laughing about?
RUBIN:	Oh, come, Mr. Higgins!
BRICE:	Oh come, Mr. Higgins.
RUBIN:	Children are like precious jewels.
BRICE:	See, daddy?
RUBIN:	Life should mean nothing without them.
BRICE:	Yeah.
RUBIN:	In the morning, the five of them dash in and I'm refreshed by their lyrical laughter. Then at breakfast,

	the pleasure of their childish games, and when I come home at night, they begin to ply me with their endless questions, then more questions, (GRADUALLY WORKS INTO A RAGE) constant questions, questions — nothing but questions! It's enough to drive a man nuts!
BRICE:	(LAUGHS) Waaaaahhhh!
FATHER:	What are you yelling about?
BRICE:	He's crazy, daddy.
FATHER:	Not as crazy as you think. What about my tickets, brother?
RUBIN:	I'm sorry, sir. Here they are. Would you like to look over your quarters?
BRICE:	I wanna quarter, daddy.
FATHER:	Keep quiet. Yes — I'd like to see the boat. Where is it?
RUBIN:	Pier Fourteen. I hope you have a pleasant trip, Mr. Higgins.
FATHER:	What are you insinuating!
BRICE:	(COYLY) You know! I think I'll tell mummy.
FATHER:	Why you — you little fifth columnist! Come on — before I give you a sound thrashing!
SOUND:	(DOOR OPENS AND CLOSES)
BRICE:	Why do they wear those strings around their —
FATHER:	You mind your own business! And I'll thank you not to mention that picture anymore!
BRICE:	You're welcome, daddy.
FATHER:	The very idea!
BRICE:	The very idea.
FATHER:	Stop aping me! I can see what kind of vacation I'm

	going to have! Finally get a chance to go to Honolulu and I have to take you!
BRICE:	And mummy.
FATHER:	Yes. (MUTTERS) Like taking a ham sandwich to a banquet!
BRICE:	Huh?
FATHER:	Nothing! Where the dickens is Pier Fourteen?
BRICE:	There's the boat, daddy!
FATHER:	Oh yes. Be careful going up the gangplank. Don't run, Snooks!
BRICE:	You afraid I'll fall in the water?
FATHER:	It's too much to hope for — but don't run, nevertheless!
NELSON:	Just a minute, little girl.
BRICE:	Who are you?
NELSON:	I'm the deck steward.
FATHER:	It's all right, Steward, I have the tickets. I'd like to see our cabin.
BRICE:	I wanna see the dancing girls.
NELSON:	May I look at your tickets, please.
FATHER:	Here.
NELSON:	Room One Forty-Four, B Deck. Follow me, please.
BRICE:	What's that long pole for, daddy?
FATHER:	That's the radio antenna.
NELSON:	No, it isn't — that's the crow's nest.
BRICE:	Where's the crow?
NELSON:	There isn't any crow.

BRICE: Why?

NELSON: Because the crow's nest on a boat isn't really a crow's nest — it's not even a nest and it has nothing to do with crows.

BRICE: Do you feel all right, mister?

NELSON: I feel fine, thank you.

BRICE: Well, what's on that long pole?

NELSON: I told you — it's a crow's nest.

BRICE: I wanna see the crow.

NELSON: There's no crow.

FATHER: You weren't satisfied when I told her it was a radio antenna, wise guy!

NELSON: I can't help it! It's the crow's nest and the child should know it!

BRICE: Yeah. Where's the crow?

NELSON: My dear child, the crow is nowhere near the nest. When the boat gets under way, a sailor will climb up there!

BRICE: To get the crow's eggs?

NELSON: No! No eggs.

BRICE: Why?

NELSON: Forgive me, sir. Now that I look closely at it, I see it's the radio antenna.

FATHER: That's better.

NELSON: Here's your cabin, sir. And here are your tickets.

BRICE: I wanna hold the tickets, daddy.

FATHER: No — they're too valuable!

BRICE:	I wanna hold the tickets!
FATHER:	Well, all right — just till we get off the boat. And don't lose them!
BRICE:	I won't.
NELSON:	Would you like to look at the bathroom, sir?
FATHER:	Yes, please. Hmmm, pretty classy cabin. Don't jump on those beds, Snooks! I'll be out in a minute.
NELSON:	This suite has both shower and tub. I think you'll find it quite comfortable, sir.
FATHER:	I'm quite sure I will. Well, thanks. Snooks!
BRICE:	Here I am, daddy. Are we going home now?
FATHER:	Yes, come along. Say goodbye to the deck steward.
BRICE:	I don't wanna. He's a pickle puss.
NELSON:	Goodbye, dear.
FATHER:	Give me the tickets, Snooks … (PAUSE) Snooks — where are the tickets?
BRICE:	I got a secret, daddy.
FATHER:	Snooks!
BRICE:	I was afraid I'd lose them — so —
FATHER:	Yes?
BRICE:	I hid them.
FATHER:	Where did you hide them?
BRICE:	In the room.
FATHER:	Let's go back quick! Where did you put them?
BRICE:	Right there. In that little cupboard with the glass door.
FATHER:	Cupboard! Ohh! That's the porthole!

BRICE: (LAUGHS) Ain't I smart, daddy?

FATHER: You little — (SLAP)

BRICE: WAAAAAAHHHHH!

NELSON: Give her one for me, too!

FATHER: You bet I will! (SLAP)

BRICE: WAAAAAAHHHHH!

NELSON: (LAUGHS LIKE A MADMAN)

FATHER: Well — there goes my vacation! Nuts! Come on!

(MUSIC … APPLAUSE)

POWELL: Thank you, Baby Snooks, daddy, and company. More of them later, ladies and gentlemen, but now, I see my number flashing in the rack. It's my pleasure to sing for you one of the newest of the torchies; a tuneful item called "Fools Rush In. "Be an angel, Meredith, and tread on it for me, will you?

"FOOLS RUSH IN" —POWELL & ORCHESTRA

(APPLAUSE)

HULL: Friends, if you haven't tried Maxwell House lately … believe me … you've got something to look forward to.

For with extra-flavored, highland-grown coffees now blended into every pound, the celebrated Maxwell House blend is richer, more fragrantly full-bodied than ever before.

And yet, it's selling today at the lowest prices ever … prices the most modest budget can afford.

More people enjoy Maxwell House today than ever before in its history. And so, it's with real gratitude to you, our friends that we look forward in September to the beginning of the ninth year of Thursday evening broadcasts for Maxwell House Coffee.

	It's been possible only because of your continued loyalty to Maxwell House. And when we meet again in September, we hope you'll find even greater enjoyment in these programs sent to you by the coffee that's now, more than ever, good to the last drop.
POWELL:	And if Warren says it, folks — it's so! Now here's something I think you'll enjoy. A few weeks ago, I did a little number called "The Breeze and I." Tonight, our lovely Maxwell House chanteuse, petite Mary Martin, will show you how the song should really have been sung.
MARTIN:	Dick, your courtliness is superseded only by your modesty.
POWELL:	I'm sincere, Mary. Now, if you'll dish it out in the Martin manner, I'll sit down and take a lesson. If you please, maestro.

"THE BREEZE AND I" —MARTIN & ORCHESTRA

(APPLAUSE)

POWELL:	What did I tell you — she's great, isn't she? Well, now comes Baby Snooks with another of her animal compositions. Bring her on, daddy.
STAFF:	Thanks, Dick. All right, Snooks — start reading.
BRICE:	Awight, daddy … Composition on the camel. The camel is the funniest animal in the world. He's got feet like a duck, a face like a moose, and a body like a rollercoaster. The camel looks awful — but he is a noble animal. He also has a noble smell. Camels live in the desert and they are very smart. They make coats, brushes, and cigarettes.
STAFF:	They do nothing of the kind!
BRICE:	Why?
STAFF:	I'll explain later. Keep on reading.

BRICE: Some camels have two humps and some camels have one hump. The ones with two humps look like a cow upside down. You can ride on their backs but you must sit between the two humps, otherwise, it will tickle you. I hope you get the point. Camels are the only animal in the world that can live for thirty days without water. I don't believe it.

STAFF: Well, it happens to be true!

BRICE: But you said Uncle Louie didn't touch water for thirty years.

STAFF: Never mind that! Finish your composition! And tell that joke.

BRICE: Awight. My daddy told me a little joke about camels. He said they never get hungry on the desert because they can always eat the sand-␣which-is there. I think that joke smells as bad as the camel. The end.

(APPLAUSE)

POWELL: That was swell, Snooks. Not long ago, a show was produced here in Hollywood that was an instantaneous smash. It had a lot of new faces, fresh young talent, and good up-to-the-minute songs. The show is called "Meet the People" — and we've picked one of its outstanding numbers to present to you for the first time on the air. It expresses the feeling of most Americans and we really get a great kick out of singing it. We offer "The Bill of Rights. "

"BILL OF RIGHTS" —POWELL & MARTIN

(APPLAUSE)

POWELL: Thank you. Well, as I told you at the beginning of the program, we're going to leave you for five weeks —

BRICE: Oh, Mr. Powell.

POWELL: Yes, Snooks?

BRICE:	Will you call all the people? I got some presents for you.
POWELL:	Isn't that sweet! Meredith! Warren! Mary! (AD LIB, WHAT'S GOING ON, ETC.)
STAFF:	All right, Snooks. Give out your presents and make it snappy.
BRICE:	Miss Martin. Here's what I got for you.
MARTIN:	A doll! Well, I never!
BRICE:	No good?
MARTIN:	Why it's wonderful! But, Snooks — I haven't played with dolls for years. I really wouldn't know what to do with it.
BRICE:	You could give it to me, if you like.
POWELL:	That's a good idea. What have you got for us, Snooks?
BRICE:	Well, I bought this lollipop for Uncle Meredith —
POWELL:	My! What a sucker!
BRICE:	Yeah — ain't he?
MERE:	It's a nice lollipop, Snooks — but I never eat candy.
BRICE:	I know — that's why I bought it for you.
STAFF:	There's method in her madness.
POWELL:	Okay — you keep the lollipop, too, Snooks. Now, what have you got for me?
BRICE:	Well, I wasn't sure whether you'd like a sweater or a fishing rod —
POWELL:	Yes?
BRICE:	So, I bought you this little electric stove.
POWELL:	Now you're cooking with electricity! You get the stove, too, Snooks.

BRICE:	(LAUGHS) Ain't I lucky, daddy?
STAFF:	Yes, very. Well, what have you got for your old dad?
BRICE:	A great big kiss! (KISSES HIM)
STAFF:	(LAUGHS) My baby! Come on, Snooks — so long everybody!
BRICE:	Goodbye! See you next month.
	(INTO FINISH)
POWELL:	Yes, friends, it's vacation time and all of us on Good News are going away for the month of August. But we'll be back with you at this same time five weeks from tonight, September 5, all ready to entertain you for Maxwell House for another season. You will hear Fanny Brice as Baby Snooks, Hanley Stafford as Daddy, Meredith Willson and his orchestra, the chorus, Mary Martin, and your humble servant, Dick Powell.
	("ALWAYS AND ALWAYS" FADES FOR)
HULL:	For another big half-hour of fun, stay tuned to this network for the "Aldrich Family," which follows immediately over most of these same stations.
	Until Thursday, September 5th then, this is Warren Hull bidding you goodnight and good luck for the makers of Maxwell House — the coffee that's always — good to the last drop!
	(MUSIC FULL AND OUT ON CUE)
NBC ANN:	Now … important news … about your favorite corn flakes!
	Post Toasties are now enriched with *vitamin B-1* … the *energy* vitamin authorities say we all need *every day*!
	Lack of vitamin B-1 may cause fatigue, poor appetite, and nervousness. Growing children, *especially* need vitamin B-1! Now Post Toasties and *no other corn flakes*

give you this *extra* value at *no extra cost.*

So tomorrow, start serving *your* family crisp, delicious Post Toasties *every day.*

This is the National Broadcasting Company.

MAXWELL HOUSE COFFEE
Presents
"LET'S LAUGH, LET'S SING"

HULL: Maxwell House Coffee presents "Let's Laugh, Let's Sing."

(STARTS WITH "ROCK-A-BY BABY," WHICH BLENDS INTO "THOUGHTS WHILE STROLLING," FADING IMMEDIATELY FOR)

HULL: Ladies and gentlemen, this is Warren Hull inviting you to spend an evening at home with Maxwell House and a brand new program fashioned for the enjoyment of all. Let's laugh with America's most famous imp, that inimitable, lovable, unpredictable little demon. Fanny Brice as Baby Snooks, with Hanley Stafford as Daddy — and let's sing with Meredith Willson and his Maxwell House orchestra as he plays the songs America sings, the simple, lovable tunes of everyday life. Melodies as homey as the clock on the mantle, bubbling up like the laughter of the younger generation — truly, the folk songs of tomorrow.

SNOOKS: Daddy!

DADDY: Quiet, Snooks. The man is talking.

SNOOKS: I wanta talk.

DADDY: Not now, later.

SNOOKS: What are you doing?

DADDY: I'm very busy working on an application.

SNOOKS: What's an applecation?

DADDY: The thing I'm working on!

SNOOKS: What are you working on?

DADDY: (YELLS) I told you, an application! I'm filling out a form. I'm trying to get insurance.

SNOOKS: What's insurance?

DADDY: Listen, Snooks, if I tell you what insurance is, will you promise not to ask any more questions?

SNOOKS: I promise.

DADDY: All right. (VERY QUICKLY) Insurance is protection for a man's family in the event of a calamity. Okay?

SNOOKS: (RAPIDLY) Okay! What's a calamity?

DADDY: Snooks, you promised —

SNOOKS: Is it a baby clam?

DADDY: Yes! Now let me alone!

SNOOKS: (LAUGHS)

(CHORD)

HULL: Well, it looks like daddy is going to be in trouble. But we'll try to keep Snooks quiet long enough for Meredith Willson to present the real thing in American music — nothing spectacular, no fancy arrangements, but the simple, lovable tunes of everyday life. But first —

(INSERT COMMERCIAL PAGE 3)

HULL: Ladies and gentlemen, the folk songs of tomorrow … the songs America sings.

"RED SAILS IN THE SUNSET" —ORCHESTRA

"REMEMBER ME" —ORCHESTRA

"I'M IN THE MOOD FOR LOVE" —STEVENS & ORCHESTRA

"THE GIRL IN THE LITTLE GREEN HAT" —ORCHESTRA

"JUST ONE MORE CHANCE" —GERMAIN & ORCHESTRA

"I LOVE LOUISA" —ORCHESTRA

"SLEEPY TIME GAL" —ORCHESTRA

"IT'S A SIN TO TELL A LIE" —ORCHESTRA

"WE JUST COULDN'T SAY GOODBYE" —ORCHESTRA

(APPLAUSE)

HULL: Yes, these are the songs America sings. Nine all-time favorites, nine grand tunes you will never forget. I'm sure most of you remembered "Red Sails in the Sunset," "Remember Me," "I'm in the Mood for Love," "The Girl in the Little Green Hat," "Just one more Chance," "I Love Louisa," "Sleepy Time Gal," "It's a Sin to Tell a Lie," and "We Just Couldn't Say Goodbye."

ANNOUNCER: And now, ladies and gentlemen, here is Fanny Brice as Baby Snooks!

(MUSIC … APPLAUSE)

ANNOUNCER: Well, daddy, played by Hanley Stafford, has decided to try and get some insurance. They rejected him a few weeks ago on account of his blood pressure but he has been watching himself closely and today, he feels confident. As the scene opens, we find daddy in his study talking to the insurance doctor. Listen.

FATHER: I hope I can pass this time, doctor.

DOC: I think you'll be all right, Mr. Higgins. It's just that your blood pressure was a little high last time I examined you.

FATHER: Yes. But since then I've taken your advice — I don't let anything excite me.

DOC: Good. Now, if you'll just fill out this form while I get cleaned up. I have to give you a thorough examination, you know.

FATHER:	Okay, doc. You can wash right down the hall.
DOC:	Right. Now just relax. I'll be back in a couple of minutes.
FATHER:	(LAUGHS) You won't find my blood pressure high this time. No sir!
SOUND:	(DOOR CLOSES)
FATHER:	Now, let's have a look at this form. Hmmm. Print name — age — place of birth. Hmmm.
SOUND:	(DOOR OPENS)
BRICE:	Hello, daddy.
FATHER:	Oh, Snooks. You'll have to leave me alone for a few minutes, dear.
BRICE:	Why?
FATHER:	The doctor's here and he's going to examine me.
BRICE:	Are you sick, daddy?
FATHER:	No, I feel fine. I'm trying to get some insurance.
BRICE:	What's insurance?
FATHER:	Insurance is a form of saving. As long as I live, I pay money to the company and if anything happens to me, the company gives the money to my beneficiary.
BRICE:	Why does he get it?
FATHER:	Why does who get it?
BRICE:	Benny Fisher.
FATHER:	I didn't say Benny Fisher. I said beneficiary. And now Snooks, can I ask you to go out and play?
BRICE:	Uh-huh. You can ask me, daddy.
FATHER:	Well, I'm asking.

BRICE:	I ain't going.
FATHER:	That's fine. Look here, Snooks. I mustn't lose my temper today.
BRICE:	Why?
FATHER:	Because my blood pressure will go up. If that happens, they won't give me any insurance.
BRICE:	What's blood pressure?
FATHER:	Did you ever see my face get red and my veins stand out?
BRICE:	Uh-huh.
FATHER:	Well, that's caused by a contraction of the blood vessels and arteries when there's any emotional excitement that results in hypertension.
BRICE:	Is it?
FATHER:	Yes. It's very complicated but it can be compared to a freezing pipe. You've seen the pipes sometimes in the winter when they freeze up and no water can get through. Then we have to send for the plumber.
BRICE:	Uh-huh.
FATHER:	Well, the same thing happens in my body — and you know the result.
BRICE:	You send for the plumber?
FATHER:	No — I send for the doctor. He's here now and you'll have to go.
BRICE:	Well, what's blood pressure?
FATHER:	I just told you! Why does my face get red?
BRICE:	Cause you holler at me.
FATHER:	That's right, and I don't want to holler at you right now! Just go away and let me fill out this form.

BRICE: What form?

FATHER: This paper I have is an application for insurance. I must answer all these questions before the doctor examines me.

BRICE: I wanna help you.

FATHER: I don't need your help. Just leave me alone. Let me see … (READS) Weight at birth … I guess it was nine pounds.

BRICE: Was you so little, daddy?

FATHER: Little? That's big! Oddly enough, when my father was born, he only weighed two pounds.

BRICE: Did he live?

FATHER: No … (READS) Mother's maiden name —

BRICE: Daddy?

FATHER: Yes?

BRICE: Do they have to weigh all the babies when they're born?

FATHER: Yes.

BRICE: Why?

FATHER: I don't know. All I know is that they weigh them before you take them home.

BRICE: Do you have to pay for them by the pound?

FATHER: I guess so. Let me finish this, Snooks. Contagious dis—

BRICE: Daddy?

FATHER: What is it?

BRICE: Has Uncle Louie got any babies?

FATHER: No!

BRICE: My teacher ain't got any babies.

FATHER:	I can't help it.
BRICE:	Why?
FATHER:	Ahhh — leave me alone. Snooks, don't you want me to have any insurance?
BRICE:	Uh-uh. What's insurance?
FATHER:	I told you. It's a protection against trouble. I have a wife and children so I must be protected against trouble.
BRICE:	When did you get into trouble, daddy?
FATHER:	When I got a wife and children!
BRICE:	Huh!
FATHER:	Nothing. And don't ask me any more questions — I'm starting to feel bad already.
BRICE:	Your face is getting red, daddy.
FATHER:	You see! My pressure's going up! If the doctor examines me now, I'm done! I'm cooked!
BRICE:	Don't tell him, daddy.
FATHER:	Don't worry — I won't have to tell him — he'll know.
BRICE:	Will he stick a fork in you?
FATHER:	Why should he stick a fork in me?
BRICE:	To see if you're cooked.
FATHER:	I mean I won't have a chance to get a policy! You simply have to leave this room until the doctor's through with me.
BRICE:	I won't bother you, daddy.
FATHER:	All right. Now, let me fill out this form in peace. (READS) Any member — family — mental disorders. Hmmm.
BRICE:	What is it, daddy?

FATHER: It's a sanity clause.

BRICE: Is he gonna get insurance, too?

FATHER: Who?

BRICE: Santy Clause.

FATHER: (MIMICS HER ANGRILY) Santy Clause — Santy Clause! Not Santa Clause — sanity clause. They want to know if anybody in my family is crazy.

BRICE: Ohhh … What you gonna tell 'em, daddy?

FATHER: What do you mean? I'm going to tell them the truth.

BRICE: Will they still give you the insurance?

FATHER: Of course, they will! What are you hinting at?

BRICE: I dunno.

FATHER: I wish that broken down doctor would hurry!

BRICE: Where is he, daddy?

FATHER: He went to clean up — I guess he must be taking a bath! I know my pressure's way up now.

BRICE: Your face ain't red anymore, daddy.

FATHER: Really, Snooks? Are you sure it's not red?

BRICE: No — it's purple.

FATHER: I know it! Ahh, what's the use — I'll never get that policy!

BRICE: What's a policy?

FATHER: Insurance! I've told you a thousand times! It's insurance.

BRICE: What's insurance?

FATHER: For the last time — I pay a premium to the insurance company and if anything happens, they pay me! Last

	week, this company paid ten thousand dollars for 50 broken arms.
BRICE:	What do they want the broken arms for?
FATHER:	They don't want the broken arms.
BRICE:	Then why did they buy them?
FATHER:	Nobody buys anything! Every time there's an accident, somebody is paid off. Yesterday, a man breaks his leg and gets five hundred dollars — today, somebody else breaks his neck and gets a thousand!
BRICE:	You think you'll be the lucky one tomorrow, daddy?
FATHER:	It has nothing to do with luck! For every type of accident, you get a certain amount.
BRICE:	How much?
FATHER:	Well, they give me twenty-five hundred dollars if I break both legs and sprain both knees.
BRICE:	Why?
FATHER:	Because that's insurance! And I can get a flat sum of three thousand if I waive the knees.
BRICE:	How much do you get if you wiggle your ears?
FATHER:	Why am I driving myself crazy explaining this stuff to you? Go on — go out and play!
BRICE:	I don't wanna.
SOUND:	(DOOR OPENS)
DOC:	Sorry I took so long, old man. Have you been relaxing?
FATHER:	Oh, sure!
BRICE:	Hello, mister.
DOC:	Well, hello little girl. Is this your pride and joy, Higgins?
FATHER:	That's one way of putting it. Her name is Snooks.

DOC:	How would you like to stick around and watch me take your daddy's blood pressure, Snooks?
BRICE:	Are you the plumber?
FATHER:	He's the doctor! Hurry up, doc — I can't hold out much longer.
DOC:	Okay. Just let me wrap this around your arm … You seem a little nervous — has anything happened?
FATHER:	Not a thing!
BRICE:	Not a thing.
DOC:	Good … Now let me adjust my stethoscope … Watch, Snooks — I'm going to pump your daddy's arm up.
BRICE:	(LAUGHS) Ooooooh — I like it.
DOC:	Keep your eye on this little column of silver. Now watch it rise.
SOUND:	(RHYTHMIC PUMPING SOUND)
BRICE:	It's going up, daddy!
FATHER:	Ohhhh!
DOC:	Hmmm!
BRICE:	A hundred and eighty — hundred and ninety — two hundred and twenty — (LAUGHS) It's still going up!
DOC:	That's curious!
BRICE:	Make it hit the top, daddy!
FATHER:	Wait a minute, doc. Tell me one thing!
DOC:	Certainly.
FATHER:	If my blood pressure is going up because I'm restraining myself — would it go down if I gave vent to my feelings?

DOC:	After a little while — I think so.
FATHER:	That's all I wanted to know!
BRICE:	I think I'll go now.
FATHER:	Wait a minute you! You little —
SOUND:	(SLAP)
BRICE:	Waaaaaahhhh!
FATHER:	Okay, doc — now take my pressure!
DOC:	Well I never!
BRICE:	Waaaaaahhhh!
	(MUSIC … PLAYOFF … APPLAUSE)
	(INSERT COMMERCIAL PAGE 6)
	("LET'S LAUGH, LET'S SING")
	("THOUGHTS WHILE STROLLING" BACKGROUND AS)
HULL:	Snooks and daddy will be back in a few moments, and later on in the program, we'll tell you how you can make money by simply sending in incidents that happen in your own home. But now, let's sing again the songs all America sings — the folk songs of tomorrow. Those simple tunes we can't forget.

"WITH MY EYES WIDE OPEN I'M DREAMING" —ORCHESTRA

"CALL ME UP SOME RAINY AFTERNOON" —ORCHESTRA

"DON'T BLAME ME" —STEVENS & ORCHESTRA

"THE OLD KITCHEN KETTLE" —ORCHESTRA

"WILD HONEY" —GERMAIN & ORCHESTRA

"CONSTANTINOPLES" —ORCHESTRA

"AM I BLUE" —ORCHESTRA

"BEAUTIFUL LADY IN BLUE" —ORCHESTRA

"OH HOW I LONG TO BELONG TO YOU" —ORCHESTRA

(APPLAUSE)

HULL: And such are the songs America sings — simple, lovable tunes of everyday life presented by Meredith Willson and his orchestra and our vocalists — Kay St. Germain and Bob Stevens.

Did you remember, "With My Eyes Wide Open I'm Dreaming," "Call Me up Some Rainy Afternoon," "Don't Blame Me," "The Old Kitchen Kettle," "Wild Honey," "Constantinople," "Am I Blue?," "Beautiful Lady in Blue," and "Oh, How I Long to Belong to You?"

In just a moment, we will hear again from Baby Snooks and we will give you the details of radio's newest and simplest contest —

(INSERT COMMERCIAL PAGE 8)

(PLAY OFF)

HULL: And now, ladies and gentlemen, here's how you can make one hundred dollars from incidents that happen in your own home. All you have to do is write to us the bright sayings of your child or children. Address your letter to Maxwell House Coffee, Battle Creek Michigan.

The Maxwell House people will turn over your suggestions to a committee of judges, including Jack Benny, Kate Smith, and Fanny Brice herself, and of course, the decisions of the judges will be final. In case of ties, duplicate prizes will be awarded.

Now for tonight's bright saying of your child. We present Mrs. George D. Williams' contribution, which Snooks and her daddy will act out now.

SNOOKS: I wanta get married.

DADDY: You can't get married.

SNOOKS: Why?

DADDY:	Because you got plenty of time to think about marrying. When you grow up to be twenty or twenty-one, you'll meet a nice young man, you'll fall in love with him, and you'll get married.
SNOOKS:	I don't wanta marry him.
DADDY:	Why not?
SNOOKS:	I wanta marry Uncle Camebert.
DADDY:	Snooks, why on earth do you want to marry Uncle Camebert?
SNOOKS:	Well — Aunt Sophie married Uncle Louie …
DADDY:	Yes?
SNOOKS:	And grandma married grandpa …
DADDY:	Yes?
SNOOKS:	And mama married you …
DADDY:	Well, what of it?
SNOOKS:	Why should I marry a stranger?
DADDY:	Ahhh … what's the use!

(PLAY OFF)

Don't forget — the bright sayings of your child may bring you one hundred dollars. Remember — simply write to Maxwell House Coffee, Battle Creek, Michigan, the bright saying of your child and the selection will be made not from the wording of your letter but from the idea contained therein.

And now, until next week, remember — "Let's Laugh, Let's Sing." This is Warren Hull saying goodnight and good luck from the makers of Maxwell House Coffee — the coffee that is always — Good to the last drop.

(APPLAUSE … THEME)

This is the National Broadcasting Company.

"LITTLE OLIVE"

An Ad-divertissement in three acts, designed for Philip Morris

[A script dated February 7, 1952, written by Phil to try to get television interest in Snooks. Considering the fact that Fanny Brice died the previous year, it's difficult to fathom who could ultimately play the annoying brat. It's especially interesting to see how times have changed—nothing wrong with talking ciggies with your kid 50 years ago! While the script seems to suddenly end, this is all that Rapp apparently wrote.]

CAST

DADDY — A long-suffering parent who sired
LITTLE OLIVE — A seven-year-old female child. The clinching argument in favor of birth control.

The entire action takes place in a modestly furnished living room. A television set is prominently featured.

FADE IN

LIVING ROOM FULL SHOT

Daddy is consulting the television page newspaper. He is walking across the room, heading for the television set, and blindly steps on a roller skate which LITTLE OLIVE has quite naturally left in the middle of the living room floor. DADDY goes down with a thud. He glares at the offending skate and mutters something unintelligible, but easily understandable to even a novice lip reader.

DADDY
(with quiet venom, audibly)
Little Olive.

At the sound of her name LITTLE OLIVE enters. She is clothed in pajamas known as Dr. Dentons. Apparently she has witnessed DADDY'S accident for she has a broad smile on her demonical little face.

OLIVE
What happened, daddy?

DADDY
(seething)
How many times have I told you not to leave your roller skates in the living room? I almost broke my neck!

OLIVE
You didn't fall on your neck — you fell on you —

DADDY
I know where I fell: And what are you doing out of bed?

OLIVE
Does everybody get more pleasure out of a Philip Morris?

DADDY
I suppose so — they sell millions of 'em.

OLIVE
It's a great racket, ain't it, daddy?

DADDY
It's not a racket at all! It just happens to be a better cigarette. Look.
    (he exhales the smoke thru his nose)
See what I did?

OLIVE
Yeah — you're smoking with you nose.

DADDY
Well, I can't do that with other cigarettes.

OLIVE
Why do you want to do it at all?

DADDY
I don't want to do it. I just wanted to show you that a Philip Morris Cigarette doesn't irritate — the others do.

OLIVE
The others do what?

DADDY
Irritate! I can smoke fifty of these a day and I never have a stale taste in my mouth.

OLIVE
Why should you if you smoke it with your nose?

DADDY
I don't smoke it with my nose! I was just demonstrating like the man does on television.

OLIVE
What man?

DADDY
The man who yaks about how good they are.

OLIVE
What's good?

DADDY
Philip Morris!

OLIVE
Is that his name?

DADDY
Whose name?

OLIVE
The man who yaks.

DADDY
No — he's just an announcer. Philip Morris is the name of a cigarette! Here it is, written right on the package! Look at it!
(he thrusts it under her nose)
See — Philip Morris & Co. Ltd., Inc.! Finest selection — special blend. Can you read it?

OLIVE
Uh-huh.

DADDY
Established over a hundred years!

OLIVE
What does that mean?

DADDY
These cigarettes are over a hundred years old.

OLIVE
Ain't they stale by now?

DADDY
I'm not talking about the cigarettes in this pack — I mean the Philip Morris Company. They've been making these cigarettes for over a hundred years. Why am I telling you all this? Why don't you go to bed?

OLIVE
I'm not sleepy, daddy. I wanna see the end.

DADDY
What end?

OLIVE
The badger lady's end

DADDY
It's too late — I'll tell you how it ends. The girl will get trapped by ——

OLIVE
No, no, no — don't tell me — I wanna see it.

DADDY
You can't see it! Go to bed this minute!

OLIVE
I'll hold my breath till my face turns blue.

And she does so.

                    DADDY
                  (alarmed)
    Stop it! All right — all right — I'll let you see it.

He goes to the set, turns on the switch. Olive relaxes her features and jumps into Daddy's chair. Daddy glares at her as he resigns himself to seat on the floor.

                    DADDY
              (between his teeth)
       Now I know why tigers eat their young.

CAMERA MOVES IN to television screen and the program is resumed.

RACKET SQUAD is over and the CAMERA PULLS back from the television screen. OLIVE is fast asleep in DADDY'S lap. He gets up with her, carrying her very gently.

                    DADDY
                   (quietly)
       Now, if I can only get her in bed without waking
       her up.

He starts to tiptoe out, gingerly.

                    OLIVE
               (opening one eye)
         Did the badger lady get caught, daddy?

                    DADDY
       Yes, she got caught. Keep your eyes closed, Olive.
       I'll have you in bed in a minute.

                    OLIVE
       I ain't sleeping.

                    DADDY
       You are, too! You slept all the way thru the last
       part.

                    OLIVE
       The last part of what?

DADDY
Of Racket Squad.

OLIVE
What's Racket Squad?

DADDY
The Philip Morris program.

OLIVE
Was he on it?

DADDY
Was who on it?

OLIVE
Philip Morris.

DADDY
Olive, I told you fifty times Philip Morris is a cigarette. Philip Morris is the company that puts on the program.

OLIVE
What program?

DADDY
Racket Squad.

OLIVE
I wanna see it.

DADDY
You can't see it — it's all over. It doesn't go on again until next week.

OLIVE
Can I see it next week?

DADDY
If you're a good girl.

OLIVE
I don't have to be a good girl — I seen it this week.

DADDY
Rubbish — you had your eyes closed all the way thru.

OLIVE
But I didn't have my ears closed. I know everything that happened.

DADDY
Well, what happened?

OLIVE
The badger lady rented the apartment to a lot of different people and she got money from Eliot and she got caught by Captain Braddock and they took her away to jail.

DADDY
I'll be darned! Well, anyway — you should have learned something from that program, Olive.

OLIVE
I did, daddy.

DADDY
Well, I don't mind you staying up a little longer if you get a good object lesson — and if it'll help make you a better citizen. What did you learn, Olive?

OLIVE
I learned that Philip Morris cigarettes are milder because they're less irritating, and that you never have a stale nose or a dry throat, and you get more smoking pleasure out of a Philip Morris because —

DADDY
Oh, for heavens sake! Come on to bed!

And he yanks her out of the room.

FADE OUT

OLIVE
I'm afraid to stay there, daddy. There's a mouse in my room.

DADDY
(getting up)
There's no mouse in your room.

OLIVE
There is too a mouse I heard him squeak.

DADDY
Well, what do you want me to do — go up and oil it? Now go on back to bed before I lose my temper with you.

OLIVE
What are you gonna do, daddy?

DADDY
(restrained)
Listen, Olive — I put in eleven hours at the office today, my boss cut my salary, your mother burned the dinner — so if it's all right with you, I'd like to watch television for an hour.

OLIVE
Why?

DADDY
Because it relaxes me. Go to bed.

OLIVE
What are you gonna watch, daddy?

DADDY
(turning on the set)
Racket Squad.

OLIVE
Is it a tennis game?

DADDY
No, it's not a tennis game. It's a different kind of

racket. This is a Philip Morris program.

> OLIVE

Oooh, I like him.

> DADDY

It's not him!

> OLIVE

Is it a her?

> DADDY

No! Philip Morris is the name of a cigarette and they put on a program called Racket Squad.

> OLIVE

Why?

> DADDY

To sell cigarettes.

> OLIVE

Is it a racket?

> DADDY

They have nothing to do with rackets! They just put the program on and you're supposed to sit back and relax and enjoy yourself.

> OLIVE

Then why ain't you doing it?

> DADDY
> (fooling with the set)

Because you won't let me. Now go to bed before I really get mad and give you a spanking ... Why won't this thing warm up? I just paid that thieving television man seven dollars to replace the condenser, and overhaul the vibrator or whatever you call it and it still doesn't work!

> OLIVE

Why don't you plug it in, daddy?

DADDY
(sees the unplugged cord)
Oh.
(he plugs it in)
Goodnight, Olive

OLIVE
Can I watch?

DADDY
No! I said you're to go to bed at once!

OLIVE
I'm thirsty.

DADDY
(twirling the dials)
Get yourself a drink. There's some beer in the icebox. I mean milk! Goodnight.

OLIVE
Goodnight, daddy.

DADDY
(settling in chair)
Good night.

OLIVE
(turns a back)
Daddy.

DADDY
What is it now?

OLIVE
I didn't do all my homework.

DADDY
Well, leave it here — I'll finish it after I see Racket Squad.

OLIVE
It's geography. I think I missed one question.

DADDY
Well, hurry up — what is it?

OLIVE
What's the shape of the earth?

DADDY
What did you put down?

OLIVE
Flat.

DADDY
That's the condition — that's not the shape. Listen, Olive, I've gone over that fifty times with you! You know the shape of the earth.

OLIVE
Do I?

DADDY
Yes, you do. What's the shape of my cuff links?

OLIVE
Square.

DADDY
Those are the cuff links I wear on Sundays! What's the shape of the cuff links I wear on weekdays?

OLIVE
Round.

DADDY
All right — now what's the shape of the earth?

OLIVE
Round on weekdays and square on Sundays.

DADDY
Okay — put that down. Goodnight, Olive.

OLIVE
Goodnight, daddy.

She leaves. CAMERA MOVES IN on television screen for standard opening to RACKET SQUAD.

At conclusion of first act of RACKET SQUAD CAMERA PULLS BACK to reveal DADDY contentedly sitting in his armchair. Directly behind the chair, squatting, is LITTLE OLIVE.

> DADDY
> Pretty good.

> OLIVE
> Yeah — it was wonderful.

Daddy leaps out of his chair, startled.

> DADDY
> Olive! Have you been down here all the time?

> OLIVE
> No, only since the program started.

> DADDY
> (turning off the set)
> Didn't I tell you I'd spank you if you didn't go to bed?

> OLIVE
> I wanna see what happens with the pretty lady, daddy.

> DADDY
> She'll get thrown in jail that's all.

> OLIVE
> Why?

> DADDY
> Because she's a crook. That's the badger game.

> OLIVE
> Can I play?

> DADDY
> It's not the kind of a game you play. She's got a racket!

OLIVE

I play with a racket.

DADDY

I told you before — this is a different kind of a racket.

OLIVE

Like Philip Morris?

DADDY

Philip Morris doesn't have any racket. They make cigarettes.

OLIVE

Why?

DADDY

So people can smoke. Go to bed, Olive.

OLIVE

Do you smoke?

DADDY

Yes.

OLIVE

Smoke to me, daddy.

DADDY

All right, I'll smoke to you. But you've got to go right to sleep after I finish this cigarette.
(He lights a Philip Morris)

OLIVE

Is it good, Daddy?

DADDY
(enjoying his cigarette)

It's great

OLIVE

Let me try it.

DADDY
Don't be silly. Little girls don't smoke.

OLIVE
Do big girls smoke?

DADDY
Some of them.

OLIVE
Does that badger lady smoke?

DADDY
I don't now — I don't remember.

OLIVE
Can I smoke when I grow up?

DADDY
When you grow up you can do as you please.

OLIVE
Then I wanna be a badger lady!

DADDY
You would! Getting more like your mother every day. Now, go to bed — I'm finished with my cigarette.

OLIVE
No, smoke some more, daddy. You said it was good.

DADDY
It is good.

OLIVE
Why?

DADDY
Because it's a Philip Morris.

OLIVE
Does that make it good?

DADDY
I don't know if it makes it good or bad. All I
know is I get more pleasure out of Philip Morris.

"UNCLE HITCHY AND LITTLE ALFRED"

[While there is no date for this script, it was probably concocted around the time of Alfred Hitchcock's hit television show, hoping to launch Snooks into the new medium of sight *and* sound. Of course, most of the humor was still done with dialogue. But was it meant as the pilot to a complete TV series? Was Hitchcock himself approached about this weird little tale? We'll never know ...]

FADE IN: PORCINE CARICATURE ON WHITE SCREEN TO RESEMBLE HITCHCOCK

THEME MUSIC: CONSISTENT WITH "HITCHCOCK PRESENTS."

In cadence, UNCLE HITCHY ENTERS and fills his profile in silhouette. As the MUSIC ENDS he turns into CAMERA, lights up

>HITCHY
>(Hitchcock voice)
>Good evening, ladies and gentlemen, my name is Alfred Hotchkiss. Tonight we present a voyage into the dark realm of shuddering experience based on the every-day happenings of my life. Yesterday was Black Saturday — the vilest day in the annals of history since the Boxer Rebellion. My son, Little Alfred, who, for reasons known only to the insufferable child persists in calling me Uncle Hitchy, was forced upon me by his mother, my dear wife, Botenoir. With a minimum of planning and a maximum of loathing I accompanied the boy on a visit to the park–

Here his VOICE takes over as we portray the scenes indicated. LITTLE ALFRED, as may be expected, is a small replica of his father.

HITCHY'S VOICE
(over scenes)
— hence to the zoo, following which I was bludgeoned into taking him for a ride on a streetcar — a vehicle I detest. At the end of the line we debarked and we found ourselves in front of a candy store. In the window, prominently displayed, was a chocolate rabbit, the size of a small elephant. Little Alfred dragged me back as I tried to maneuver him past the shop.

ALFRED

Uncle Hitchy! I —

HITCHY

Please, Alfred! You're not to say another word.

ALFRED

Why?

HITCHY

Because I cannot stand the sound of your voice! Let's go.

ALFRED
(resisting)
No! I don't wanna! I want that rabbit.

HITCHY
(tugging at him)
Not on your life!

ALFRED

Waaahhh! I want that rabbit!

HITCHY

Stop your hysterical keening! I took you to the park and you had three tons of ice-cream. I took you to the zoo and you ate all the peanuts and crackerjacks in sight. I took you for a long streetcar ride and you ate seventeen packages of bubble gum. What more do you want?

ALFRED
I want that rabbit!

HITCHY
Well, you can't have it. You'll get sick.

ALFRED
(dizzy expression)
I *am* sick!

HITCHY
(pulling him)
Good, I'll take you to the hospital!

He whisks Alfred off

DISSOLVE

EXT. MUSEUM OF ART

Hitchy and Alfred approach the museum, Hitchy still pulling the boy.

ALFRED
I don't wanna go in no hospital.

HITCHY
It isn't the hospital — it's the Museum of Art.

ALFRED
I don't wanna go in there.

HITCHY
You're going just the same.

ALFRED
Why?

HITCHY
You told me you had to write a composition on Art.

ALFRED
Art who?

HITCHY
Art nobody! Paintings, sculpture — that's art. And the best place to learn about it is in the Museum. Come on, you little philistine, got educated!

He whisks him into the building.
INT. MUSEUM OF ART

As they enter. From a rack on the wall Hitchy takes a catalog which his hands to Alfred.

> HITCHY
> Here. This is a catalog. Study it and keep your voice low. Look at the statues.

They pass a statue of Venus. Alfred pulls Uncle Hitchy back.

> ALFRED
> (loud)
> Lookit, Uncle Hitchy.

> HITCHY
> (hisses)
> Quiet! What is it?

> ALFRED
> (pointing to Venus)
> That lady ain't got no arms.

> HITCHY
> That's what happens to little boys who bite their fingernails. Let's move.

> ALFRED
> I don't wanna. She ain't got no clothes on.

> HITCHY
> It's only a statue — and as a rule statues don't wear clothes.

> ALFRED
> She's barefoot all over.

> HITCHY
> I know it. Come on.

> ALFRED
> Why ain't she wearing any clothes, Uncle Hitchy?

HITCHY
I told you! Statues are considered more artistic without clothes.

ALFRED
Why?

HITCHY
I don't know.

ALFRED
Is it like the burlesque show?

HITCHY
What are you talking about?

ALFRED
Well, when mummy yelled at you for going to the bur —

HITCHY
Never mind that! Your mummy wouldn't know a work of art if it crawled up and bit her!

ALFRED
Did they bite you at the burl —

HITCHY
Forget about the burlesque show!

ALFRED
(still staring at Venus)
She looks just like my teacher.

HITCHY
Oh, she does not!

ALFRED
How do *you* know?

HITCHY
(Pulls him away)
Keep your voice down — people are staring at us!

ALFRED
(pointing off)
Lookit — there's Aunt Louise!

HITCHY
(looking in that direction)
Where's Aunt Louise?

POV SHOT PITHECANTHROPUS ERECTUS

BACK TO SCENE

HITCHY
That's not Aunt Louise! That's a statue of the Missing Link.

ALFRED
It looks like Aunt Louise.

HITCHY
I don't care. It's the Missing Link — and it isn't polite to shriek out loud that your Aunt Louise looks like that gruesome statue.

ALFRED
Why? Can the statue hear me?

HITCHY
No. It's only a model and it's called Pithecanthropus Erectus.

ALFRED
Why?

HITCHY
That's his scientific name. Some scientists claim that men are descended from monkeys — they've discovered the Cro-Magnon man, the Neanderthal man and — and —

ALFRED
And Aunt Louise.

HITCHY

No! And several less anthropoidal species. I don't know how it works out but they fit this thing into it somehow.

ALFRED

Which thing?

HITCHY

Aunt Louise. I mean the Missing Link! That's part of evolution.

ALFRED

What's evolution?

HITCHY

I just told you. Some people believe all men were once monkeys.

ALFRED

Do you believe it?

HITCHY

It doesn't interest me.

ALFRED

Why?

HITCHY

Because I don't care if my grandfather was an ape!

ALFRED

Did your grandmother care?

HITCHY

Oh, stop it! Why aren't you making notes?

ALFRED

Notes for what?

HITCHY

For your composition. I think you might say something about that statue. It's Redin's most famous work and it's called "Le Penseur."

ALFRED
Huh?

HITCHY
The Thinker. It's called The Thinker.

ALFRED
(laughs)
That's funny.

HITCHY
What's funny about it?

ALFRED
That's what you call Aunt Louise!

HITCHY
I have never in my life called your Aunt Louise a thinker!

ALFRED
Thinker! Oh, I thought you said —

HITCHY
Never mind what you thought I said! Just write!

ALFRED
Okay, okay,

HITCHY
(examining his catalog)
August Rodin was born in Paris in 1840 and was employed in the studio of Carriers — Belle use where he learned to deal with the mechanical difficulties of a sculptor. In 1864 his individuality was manifested in his "Man with a Broken Nose" and he soon attained recognition and international fame thru his expert use of confluent motion in bas-relief or circular plinth eschewing contemporary methods of work. Get that?

ALFRED
Uh-huh. How do you spell "work"?

HITCHY
Ahh, you're not even istening to me!

ALFRED
Well, you talk too fast.

HITCHY
Just say he was a chiseler. That's good enough.

ALFRED
Let's go in that other room.

HITCHY
No, that's the Egyptian room. There's nothing in there by mummies.

ALFRED
Mummy's what?

HITCHY
Just mummies!

ALFRED
Is mummy playing bridge in there?

HITCHY
No, No! These are Egyptian mummies.

ALFRED
Where do they keep the daddies?

HITCHY
This mummy has nothing to do with daddy!

ALFRED
I know. Because she caught you going to the burles —

HITCHY
Stop that! A mummy is a dried up bag of crumbling bones bound up in tight-fitting trappings.

ALFRED
I'm gonna tell her what you said!

HITCHY
I'm not talking about your mummy!

ALFRED
Why?

HITCHY
And if the shoe fits she can wear it! Why don't you go look at the statues and make some notes?

ALFRED
(squirming on the floor)
I wanna go home.

HITCHY
(looking at his watch)
We can't go home yet. Those buzzards are still playing bridge.

ALFRED
I wanna go home.

HITCHY
Please, Alfred, don't make a scene in here. Come on, let's enjoy these wonderful paintings then we can get out of this broken-down place.

ALFRED
I don't wanna see no painting. I wanna go home!

HITCHY
Shh! ... Oh, look at this gorgeous thing. Leda and the Swan!

ALFRED
Where?

HITCHY
This one. Isn't it beautiful?

ALFRED
Yeah. Can I touch it?

HITCHY
No, you can't touch it. Why would you want to touch it?

ALFRED
I wanna see if the swan's got real fur on it.

HITCHY
It's not fur, silly. Swans don't have fur, they have down. His whole coat is down.

ALFRED
Huh?

HITCHY
I said that swan's whole coat is down.

ALFRED
Is his pants down too?

HITCHY
Keep moving. It'll soon be time to go home.

ALFRED
What's this one, daddy? With the old lady in a chair.

HITCHY
It's called "A study in Black and White." That's a Whistler.

ALFRED
I wanna hear it whistle.

HITCHY
It can't whistle.

ALFRED
I wanna hear it whistle!!

HITCHY
That's the artist's name — Whistler! Oh, look at this gigantic mural!

FULL SHOT of a large mural painted to conform with the ensuing description.

                ALFRED'S VOICE
That's a big one, ain't it?

                HITCHY'S VOICE
It's a masterpiece. That's the celebrated "Circus Maximus" by Corot. It says there.

                BACK TO SCENE:

                ALFRED
What's them lions doing?

                HITCHY
    (gives a surreptitious glance at his catalog)
Well, that was a sport that the cruel Roman emperors used to indulge in. First they'd be entertained by the gladiators who fought and wrestled until one or the other was killed.

                ALFRED
Ohhh.

                HITCHY
Even that gory amusement wasn't enough to appease the blood-thirsty appetites of the barbarous rulers, so they'd turn loose ten or twelve of the most ferocious and hungry lions they could find — and then — into this huge arena with those lions loose they'd push some poor, innocent citizens.

                ALFRED
    (really looking worried)
Uh-huh.

                HITCHY
This painting depicts the ancient savagery in all its horrible cruelty. The grinning, hideous faces of the spectators, the ravenous, yawning jaws of the poor innocents about to be devoured.

ALFRED
(breaks down)
Waaaaahhhhhhhhh!

HITCHY
Oh, I'm sorry, Alfred. I didn't think you'd be so touched.

ALFRED
(crying)
It's awful. Uncle Hitchy.

HITCHY
I'm gratified that you're able to see evil in such fierce lust.

ALFRED
That ain't why I'm crying.

HITCHY
It's not? Then what are you crying about?

ALFRED
(pointing)
That little lion in the corner ain't getting any!

HITCHY
(disgusted)
Ahh—what's the use — come on home!

FADE OUT

BearManorMedia
PO BOX 71426 · ALBANY, GEORGIA 31708

THE PHILIP RAPP JOKE FILE
For the first time ever, be privy to the open caverns of mirth that is the prolific Philip Rapp joke file! Rapp, writer for Baby Snooks, Eddie Cantor and creator of the *Bickersons*, wrote and collected jokes for years, drawing from it during his classic radio and TV years. Now we've taken the best quips and put them together for one great and funny book! Illustrated.
ISBN: 1-59393-102-6. $14.95

NOT SO DUMB
THE LIFE AND CAREER OF MARIE WILSON
by Charles Tranberg
Ready for the first biography on blonde, bubbly Marie Wilson? Was she really that vapid? Well — read the book on this *My Friend Irma* star!
ISBN: 1-59393-049-6. $19.95

TWENTY QUESTIONS
by Robert VanDeventer
A novelized memoir of *Twenty Questions*, one of the first weekly panel quiz shows on the radio.
ISBN: 1-59393-077-1. $19.95

INCORRECT ENTERTAINMENT
by Anthony Slide
Cultural Historian Anthony Slide, who has been described by the *Los Angeles Times* as a one-man publishing phenomenon, strikes again with a book guaranteed to contain something OFFENSIVE for everyone. From FASCISM in Hollywood to the latest topical jokes on the *Challenger* disaster & more.
ISBN: 1-59393-093-3. $19.95

FRED MACMURRAY: A BIOGRAPHY
by Charles Tranberg
A biography of Hollywood's most famous dad! Features an introduction by Don Grady of *My Three Sons*. Coming in October!
ISBN: 1-59393-099-2. $24.95.

ANGELIC HEAVEN
A Fan's Guide To Charlie's Angels
by Mike Pingel
The ultimate fan's guide to the hit 70s/80s television series by legendary producer Aaron Spelling. Filled with facts about the show, behind-the-scenes tidbits, rare photos and forewords by Farrah Fawcett and Cheryl Ladd, Angelic Heaven will have you rushing out to buy the DVDs!
$19.95

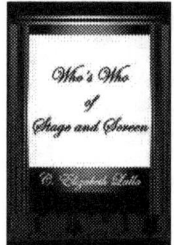

WHO'S WHO OF STAGE & SCREEN
by C. Elizabeth Lalla
Who's Who of Stage and Screen will make a beautiful addition to any Hollywood lover's collection! Filled with photos, profiles, resumes and contact information for the artists included. Nearly 600 pages, 8x10 size!
$35.00

THE FILMS OF THE DIONNE QUINTUPLETS
by Paul Talbot
An emphasis on their interesting film career of the famous five. Packed with photos and priceless information, every film fan will marvel at their story. Ships in August.
ISBN: 1-59393-097-6. $19.95.

ADD $3.00 POSTAGE FOR EACH BOOK

ORDER THESE BOOKS AND MORE! VISIT WWW.BEARMANORMEDIA.COM

www.ingramcontent.com/pod-product-compliance
Lightning Source LLC
Chambersburg PA
CBHW071432150426
43191CB00008B/1109